God the Boxer

God the Boxer

John Gimenez

Destiny Image Publishers
P.O. Box 310
Shippensburg, PA 17257-0310

"Speaking to the Purposes of God for this Generation"

ISBN 1-56043-102-4

For Worldwide Distribution
Printed in the U.S.A.

Destiny Image books are available through these fine distributors outside the United States:

Christian Growth, Inc.,
Jalan Kilang-Timor, Singapore 0315

Lifestream
Nottingham, England

Rhema Ministries Trading
Randburg, South Africa

Salvation Book Centre
Petaling, Jaya, Malaysia

Successful Christian Living
Capetown, Rep. of South Africa

Vision Resources
Ponsonby, Auckland, New Zealand

WA Buchanan Company
Geebung, Queensland, Australia

Word Alive
Niverville, Manitoba, Canada

Dedication

Every pastor needs a pastor. My pastor is David Minor.

At the recent annual convention of my home church in Coudersport, Pennsylvania, I found myself sitting next to a young man. He remarked, "Some day I want to be like Pastor Minor. I would like to have his type of ministry and be the kind of person that he is."

I turned to him and replied, "Do you understand what you're asking for? Can you begin to realize what this man has been through in order to reach the place of his ministry, character and person? If you only knew what it took to become the man of God that he is, you might not be too quick to want to become just like him."

There is a passage of scripture that describes my pastor and all that he has endured in the ministry:

Who shall ever separate us from Christ's love? Shall suffering and affliction and tribulation? Or calamity or distress? Or persecution, or hunger, or destitution, or peril, or sword?

Even as it is written, For Thy sake we are put to death all the day long, we are regarded and counted as sheep for the slaughter. [Psalm 44:2]

Yet amid all these things we are more than conquerors and gain a surpassing victory through Him Who loved us.

For I am persuaded beyond doubt—am sure—that neither death, nor life, nor angels, nor principalities, nor things impending and threatening, nor things to come, nor powers,

Nor height, nor depth, nor anything else in all creation will be able to separate us from the love of God which is in Christ Jesus our Lord.

Romans 8:35-39, *The Amplified Bible*

Years ago, the Lord gave me a vision concerning my pastor. I saw his heart, and his heart was bleeding. Like most godly shepherds, he was concerned with the sorrow, agony and pain of the sheep. His heart was broken, for the very people he loved often turned against him. These were sheep whom he nurtured, prayed over, taught and trained. Some of them suddenly left the flock without a word of farewell. Others even spoke evil of the pastor who fed them. As the vision continued, I watched the drops of blood falling from my pastor's heart. As they fell to the ground, every drop became a flower and bloomed immediately.

So it has been with this true warrior and statesman. He is a preacher who excels, a lover of God and men. I owe so much to Pastor Minor and Sister Lorraine. They took me in, gave me a place to stay, prayed over me and fed me, as they have done with other broken lives who have come to their doorstep. They reached out to me when I was in need. They have a way of just loving you, ministering to you and encouraging you. They make you look beyond your limitations and conditions to see the Christ in you and who you can become in Him.

I know how that young preacher felt. I gratefully dedicate this volume to the man of God. Like my friend at the table, "Someday I want to be like my pastor, David Minor."

Acknowledgments

To all those who have encouraged, motivated, instructed, influenced and loved me.

First of all, to my beautiful wife, Reverend Anne Gimenez, without whose help, love and spiritual insight, this book and everything else I have done would not have happened. Outside of Jesus Christ, darling, you are the strength of my life. You have no shadow of turning. You are consistent, continual, perpetual and never change. You are a woman of God with every fiber of your being. Many times my flesh has wanted to vacillate, but you have been a constant reminder of the sovereignty of God, and He has always kept me. Your total commitment, life and dedication is to God and His Son, to the Holy Spirit and to His Word.

To the many ministers who have touched my life, to Pat Robertson, Charles Green, David Schoch and others who have fought the good fight of faith for so many years. To Oral Roberts, Kenneth Copeland, Bill Bright, and many who are too numerous to mention by name, but who through friendship, the power of God, and the Word of God in their lives, have revealed more of God to me.

To Elim Bible Institute, for the work it has done in my life.

To my mother in the Lord, Reverend Leoncia Rousseau, for her love and sacrifice she made on my behalf when I first came to salvation.

To all the men and women of God who have imparted the Word of God to my life. Your teaching, preaching and words are interwoven in my spirit. You are in my heart.

To all my friends and family, especially to my children. To the local church that I pastor, and the Rock Ministerial Fellowship family of ministers that I dearly love and am honored to serve.

To my dedicated secretaries and staff, whose help and encouragement made this book a reality.

Finally, to my mother, whose love for God is unsurpassed. Mom, your sacrifice for your children can never be repaid. At eighty-five years of age, you are still preaching to all of us.

The God that Is Able

O God, we have heard with our ears,
Our fathers have told us,
The work that Thou didst in their days,
In the days of old.

Thou with Thine own hand didst drive out the nations;
Then Thou didst plant them;
Thou didst afflict the peoples,
Then Thou didst spread them abroad.

For by their own sword they did not possess the land;
And their own arm did not save them;
But Thy right hand, and Thine arm, and the light of Thy
presence,
For thou didst favor them.

Thou art my King, O God;
Command victories for Jacob.

Through Thee we will push back our adversaries;
Through Thy name we will trample down those who rise
up against us.

For I will not trust in my bow,
nor will my sword save me.

But Thou hast saved us from our adversaries,
And Thou hast put to shame those who hate us.

In God we have boasted all day long,
And we will give thanks to Thy name forever.

Psalm 44:1-8

Contents

Foreword

*For though ye have ten thousand instructors in Christ,
yet have ye not many fathers: for in Christ Jesus I have
begotten you through the gospel.*

I Corinthians 4:15

John Gimenez is a father to the Body of Christ. He is a
prophet with a message for the Church of the nineties.

God has sovereignly knit my heart to this man and his
spiritual family. Though a seasoned warrior with an internation-
al ministry, his greatest strength is his simple love for the Lord
Jesus, our Commander and Chief. This is evidently manifested
in two ways: first, his love for people, his passion for the lost;
and secondly, his teachable spirit. The greatness of this simple,
yet powerful man is the greatness of his heart. There are few
men today of his caliber and spiritual maturity who have
remained men of genuine humility, still open and willing to
hear what the Holy Spirit is presently saying to the Church.

This book is a treasury of life's experiences. It reminds me
of the old soldier, who in Second Samuel 22 and Psalm 18,
reflected back over his military career and kingly administra-
tion. As with David, the Lord has been our brother's Rock, his
buckler, and high tower. John Gimenez was taken from the

streets of New York City, drawn out of many waters, and delivered from the strong enemy. He has been brought forth into a large place and rewarded for righteousness' sake. He has kept the ways of the Lord, and his candle has been lit. He has run through a troop and leaped over a wall. God taught his hands to war, and now he is a weapon of righteousness in the hand of the Lord. Girded with strength for the battle, His gentleness has made him great.

The Lord liveth; and blessed be my rock; and let the God of my salvation be exalted.

Psalm 18:46

When I first read *God the Boxer*, I knew that it was more than a theology or a clever idea. This book is a manual for ministry, and is must reading for every young pastor. The three chapters on the unity of the Body of Christ are classic. The principles of spiritual warfare herein need to be taught in every local church. The hope revealed by the eternal victory of our Lord is like warm oil, comforting the saints. Written by a crafty veteran who has survived the war in the streets and the war in the Church, these are words which are easy to be understood, words which the Holy Ghost teaches. The spirit of this volume throughout is one who knows what it really means to be brought out of darkness into His marvelous light, one who has been forgiven much, one who loves much.

From the first bell and The Opening Rounds, we learn that we are under new management, that our fight is with principalities and powers, not one another. The Middle Rounds furnish the secrets and tactics that every boxer must know. Armed with a desire to win, knowing that the battle is the Lord's, our opponent is discerned and picked apart piece by piece. Enemies without and within are no match for the Greater One who lives within us. The Final Rounds are prophetic, emphasizing the current restoration and revival in the earth, and anticipating the fulness of the Feast of Tabernacles and the coming of our Lord!

Two kinds of preachers make me want to preach: those who can and those who can't! John Gimenez can preach, and he has stirred my heart. When I read this book the second and third times, I felt like a young lieutenant sitting across the table from a general, listening to the art of spiritual military science. These words have helped me as a Christian in my walk with the Lord, and have been a resource for me as a pastor to become a more effective servant-leader to my people.

Arise, Church! The Lord will fight for you! You are about to meet God the Boxer!

Pastor Kelley Varner, Th.B., D.D.
Senior Pastor
Praise Tabernacle
Richlands, North Carolina

Preface

It was April 12, 1963. I had just been released from serving a number of years in prison for criminal activities and drug addiction. While in jail, a fellow told me about a little church called Damascus in the Bronx, New York. He said, "John, you need to go to that church and get your life changed." I mocked him, calling him the "Billy Graham" of the Bronx County Jail. He kept saying, "You should go there. You might find God...you might even become a preacher!" Then we both laughed.

I had no place to call home. I couldn't go to my parents' place because they had given up hope that I would ever change. So I went to my old neighborhood and took a shot of dope. That night on the subway, I fell asleep, passing my intended destination. When I got off the train and walked down the street, I saw a sign, a cross that lit up the night. It said, "Iglesia Christiano Damasco," or The Damascus Christian Church!

My mind was so corrupt. I thought to myself, "I bet they're selling dope in that church. The drug pushers are using the church as a front, even with shooting galleries. I'm going up there and check it out. Maybe I can get in on what they are doing." When I went into the sanctuary, the place was full! People were praying and shouting and praising God. That night was my first encounter with the moving of the Holy Ghost. I had been brought up in church, but I had never seen what I saw that night.

The preacher spoke about a program that they had for drug addicts. That night I was permitted to stay at the church. There were no beds, so I slept in the sanctuary. The next day, they drove me to a place called Mountaindale in upstate New York. The place was filled. As soon as I got there, I wanted to leave. But I began meeting a lot of the drug addicts I had known. Something had happened to them! Their lives had been changed! Others were fighting against an experience and a move of God. In fact, four or five of them had grown a marijuana patch out in the woods.

I wanted God to do something for me. Not long after, I had a powerful encounter with Jesus Christ! He came into my life. For the first time, I was truly happy. I got filled with the Holy Ghost and went around like a man who was drunk. I felt so high, so good, I was floating on cloud nine! Praise the Lord!

Then one day I got a package from my mother. In it were some goodies and a brand new shirt. I said to myself, "I am going to put this shirt away for the special times when we get visitors." Different churches that had heard about the work at Mountaindale would visit, and many times there would be ladies in those groups. "Who knows," I thought, "there might be a young Christian lady who would be attracted to me!"

About a month later, we were advised that we were going to have company. We began to clean our rooms and get ready. I shared a room with a fellow that I had known for many years. His name was Al Sanford. We used to call him "Fat Albert" or "Fat Sanford." The visitors were due in the afternoon, so I quickly went to do my other work in the building. A couple of buses showed up at lunchtime. I thought to myself, "I'm going upstairs to take a shower and put on my new shirt." I wanted to look my best, and had even polished my shoes. But my new shirt was nowhere to be found!

I looked in all my drawers, but the shirt was not there. Finally, I put on my old things and went looking for my roommate, Fat Sanford. Perhaps he knew where my special shirt was. He wasn't downstairs, so I began to get anxious. Across the road, in a big field where we played all our sports, were about ten or fifteen guys playing football. Sure enough, there was Fat Albert, and he had my new shirt on! Only now it was dirty and had been torn. Well, I came down...I tumbled down...I crashed down from cloud nine. When I did, I landed right on top of Fat Sanford! We fought and exchanged blows. I wanted to hurt him as bad as I could. This man had taken my brand new shirt and destroyed it, along with the dreams that I once had of looking good for the visitors. Right then, I didn't care about visitors or anything else. I really lost it!

I was so angry that I decided to go back to New York City. I even went looking for the guys who had the marijuana patch. I wanted to get high again, go back into sin. I couldn't find them, so I went back to my room and began to pack my few belongings. Maybe I could hitch a ride on the visitors' bus.

In the midst of my rage and wanting to kill Fat Sanford, I heard singing from downstairs. The service had begun. That sound of praise and worship entered my mind, my heart and my spirit. I knelt with my head on the bed and began to cry. I prayed, "God, I don't want to go back to the hell, the pain, the jails, and all the shame of living as a drug addict, a leper of society. There is nothing back there for me except prison, death or insanity. Please help me, God, help me before it's too late. I don't want to go back to my old life!"

Then God spoke to me. In my spirit, His voice was so clear. I could almost see the Lord standing before me, loving me, caring for me. He said, "Do you want to win this battle? Do you want to win this warfare?" I said, "Yes, Lord, I don't want to be defeated. I want to win!" He replied, "If you really want to win the fight, then you've got to let Me be your Manager!"

I understood that! God wanted to take control of every area of my life. He had to become the Manager of my life. I had been involved in boxing and knew something about managing. God wanted to watch out for me, to decide what was best for my life. There, almost thirty years ago, in a little room in an old beat-up hotel that had become a rehabilitation center for drug addicts, I met the Lord and cried out, "Yes, Lord! You are my Manager! Manage me!"

Much has happened since that experience in Mountaindale. God has been my Manager. He has richly blessed my life, allowing me to work with Him in the ministry of the evangelist and the pastor as well as the prophetic and apostolic. I have traveled throughout the world and have talked with many great ministers and world leaders. God has taken care of me and my family.

But I have also listened to the pain and sorrow, the disappointments of many young ministers beginning in the work of the Lord. All over this nation, there are frustrated pastors whose churches have not grown. Men and women have left the ministry because of heartbreak, conflicts and a raging opponent who never lets up. I have been moved by the stories of many people who want God with all their heart, but who still seem to be in a constant conflict with their flesh.

In the past thirty years, my Manager and I have had many experiences, many highs and lows, good rounds and bad rounds. I have looked from the mountaintops and I have almost been buried in the valleys. Through it all, God has proven His sovereign love for me.

This book was born out of a multitude of encounters with the enemy and victories over him. There has been a lot of blood spilled on the battlefield. But there have also been a lot of great joys, fulfilled moments and great experiences in the wonder and beauty of holiness.

There are many conflicts yet to come. This volume was written to encourage, strengthen, motivate and warn leaders, the shepherds over God's flock. My prayerful purpose is that you will be encouraged to stand in whatever the battle is...and go all the way!

Finish the good fight!

John Gimenez

Introduction

The Opening Rounds: Under New Management

*Therefore, if any man be in Christ, he is a new creature:
old things are passed away; behold, all things are become new.*

2 Corinthians 5:17

*But ye are a chosen generation, a royal priesthood, an
holy nation, a peculiar people; that ye should shew forth
the praises of Him who hath called you out of darkness
into His marvelous light: Which in time past were not a
people, but are now the people of God: which had not
obtained mercy, but now have obtained mercy.*

1 Peter 2:9-10

*I therefore, the prisoner of the Lord, beseech you that ye
walk worthy of the vocation wherewith ye are called,*

*With all lowliness and meekness, with longsuffering, for-
bearing one another in love;*

*Endeavoring to keep the unity of the Spirit in the bond of
peace.*

*There is one body, and one Spirit, even as ye are called
in one hope of your calling;*

One Lord, one faith, one baptism,

One God and Father of all, who is above all and through all, and in you all.

Ephesians 4:1-6

The bell rings!

The moment of truth has come. Across the ring is my opponent. He is short and ugly and hairy. His lips are moving as he breathes out threatenings and cursings.

He is not a novice. This is not his first fight. He once killed a man with his bare hands. He looks dangerous! This isn't playtime. My adversary is not my sparring partner. This is for real!

All the hard work, the running, the exercising, the diet, the seeming monotony of training is behind me. Now, my time has come. I am sure of my skills and aware of my enemy's tactics. But that is not the source of my confidence. My greatest comfort is the Man in the corner with me. This may sound strange, but I know He loves me.

I am a soldier of Jesus Christ. I am a fighter and my opponent is the devil. But I have no fear. I know that my victory is assured because *God is my manager.*

God reveals Himself to us in many ways. He is Creator, Father and Provider. He is our Savior, Healer and King.

But He revealed Himself to me as *God the Boxer.*

A friend and I were giving out tracts in the mountains of Pennsylvania; when we stopped at a Mennonite farm. My friend walked up on the steps and knocked at the door, while I stood by the stairs. As he was knocking, this big old dog that looked like a baby horse came across the fields, growling deep in this throat.

He was ugly, wrinkled and mean-looking. He looked like a guy who had been in the ring for five years. My friend froze, and I got ready to run up the steps. Just as the dog neared us, the door opened, and this lady wearing a little cap on the back of her head looked at the dog and said, "Whoa, Rover!"

He stopped and stared at my friend like a hungry man looking at a plate of pork chops. But he saw that my friend was protected, standing next to that little lady who had the spirit of God in her life. My friend was standing next to "the champ." That dog was not about to do anything.

Then, all of a sudden, he spied me and looked as if he had seen a steak. He turned around and started after me, and I turned around to leave in a hurry! Just then, he opened his mouth—and he did not have one single tooth in his head. When I saw that, I lost all fear.

The devil has no more teeth. He lost them in the ring with Jesus. The Word of the Lord is true.

But Thou, O Lord, art a shield for me; my glory, and the lifter up of my head...

I will not be afraid of ten thousands of people, that have set themselves against me round about.

Arise, O Lord; save me, O my God: for Thou hast smitten all mine enemies upon the cheek bone; Thou hast broken the teeth of the ungodly.

Psalm 3:3, 6-7

God is the Champion Boxer. He has been "boxing" the devil for centuries and He beats him every time. God takes great pleasure in boxing the devil through us!

I am going to take you to a ringside seat at the greatest Championship Boxing Match of all time. You are going to see in the *opening rounds* who our opponent is and how he fights. In the *middle rounds* you will learn how to attack this challenger and the tactics and strategies that will defeat him. When we get to the final rounds, you will know the sweet taste of total victory.

But before we begin, we must come to understand the most essential requirement for winning this Championship Bout. We must be "Under New Management."

Under New Management

The word "management" means; (1) the act or manner of management or handling, controlling, directing; (2) to have charge of, direct, administer; (3) to get a person to do what one wishes; (4) to make docile or submissive.

A manager is one who sets in order the process that is to take place to achieve a goal. To be under management means that we are controlled by someone or something. Everyone and everything is under management.

Let every soul be subject unto the higher powers. For there is no power but of God; the powers that be are ordained of God.

Whosoever therefore resisteth the power, resisteth the ordinance of God; and they that resist shall receive to themselves damnation.

Romans 13:1-2

The elements of nature are under management.

Fear ye not Me? saith the Lord. Will ye not tremble at My presence, Who have placed the sand for the bound of the sea by a perpetual decree...

Jeremiah 5:22a

The beasts of the field are under management.

For we know that the whole creation groaneth and travaileth in pain together until now.

Romans 8:22

Another word for management in the Bible is "authority." The Gospels tell of a Roman centurion who understood management and order.

Wherefore, neither thought I myself worthy to come unto Thee; but say in a word, and my servant shall be healed.

*For I also am a man set **under authority**, having under me soldiers, and I say unto one, Go; and he goeth; and to another, Come; and he cometh: and to my servant, Do this; and he doeth it.*

Luke 7:7-8

Before we heard the good news of salvation through Jesus Christ, we were under the management of death.

And you hath He quickened, who were dead in trespasses and sins;

Wherein in time past ye walked.

Ephesians 2:1-2a

By the mercy of God and by a deliberate act, we must choose to submit our lives to the training, direction and control of a new Manager.

Humble yourselves, therefore, under the mighty hand of God, that He may exalt you in due time.

1 Peter 5:6

God Will Fight for You

God rules from His throne in Heaven, and Jesus is seated at His side at this moment, but that does not mean that the Godhead is passive. God is not simply "letting things happen." Jesus finished the work on the cross and in His resurrection, defeating the works of satan (1 John 3:8), but that does not mean we have fully understood or appropriated His eternal victory. The Church must walk this thing out in shoe leather. Through the Holy Spirit, God has empowered us individually and corporately to continue to clear out the enemy from our territories.

When General Douglas MacArthur and the Allied forces finally returned to the Philippine Islands during World War II, they quickly overpowered the Japanese forces holding the main islands and cities. The Allied invasion force won the main battle, but it took thousands of Allied "clean-up crews" many long and dangerous months to root out, surround and defeat every hidden pocket of resistance, every sniper and every "booby trap" left behind for unsuspecting victims. The battle had been won, but there was still a work to do. In the same way, we must always remember that Jesus defeated satan and his works so that we could defeat the adversary in our lives.

Behold, I give unto you power to tread on serpents and scorpions, and over all the power of the enemy: and nothing shall by any means hurt you.

Luke 10:19

Billy Sunday once said. "I hate the devil, and whenever I find him, I kick him with my feet, I knee him with my knee, I hip him with my hip, I elbow him with my elbow, I shove him with my shoulder, I butt him with my head, I pound him with my fist, I bite him with my teeth; and, when I'm old and gray and have no teeth, I'll gum him with my gums!"

God is a Fighter, and He wants the Church of Jesus to become just like Him. But first, we must understand spiritual warfare and have a revelation of the battlefield. Our biggest battle takes place in our own backyard—gaining victory over our own flesh.

Middle Rounds: Spiritual Warfare

For though we walk in the flesh, we do not war after the flesh:

(For the weapons of our warfare are not carnal, but mighty through God....)

2 Corinthians 10:3-4

Thou, therefore, endure hardness, as a good soldier of Jesus Christ.

No man that warreth entangleth himself with the affairs of this life; that he may please him who hath chosen him to be a soldier.

2 Timothy 2:3-4

I therefore so run, not as uncertainly; so fight I, not as one that beateth the air.

1 Corinthians 9:26

Great fighters are not born, they are made. Though they may be gifted with great potential, they will never be champions without the instruction and discipline of capable managers.

Every boxer has a "corner team." He has a *manager* who plans every aspect of his training and continually tells him what strategy to use and what actions to take. He has a *"cut man"* who massages his muscles, treats his bruises and heals his cuts. He also has a *handler* who works with him on a day-to-day basis, disciplining his body, training his mind and honing his skills.

Under our "new management" we also have a "corner team"—the Father, Son and Holy Spirit. They have designed a custom-made training program to bring each of us to our full potential. The process is not easy—there is no room for self-indulgence. It is going to cost us our pride, our ambition and our favorite sins. But it is worth it.

Our Manager knows the big picture. He knows our adversary's strengths and weaknesses. He knows how to defeat him.

A great fighter *listens* to his manager.

Final Rounds: Winning the Prize

Fear not, O land. Be glad and rejoice; for the Lord will do great things...

Be glad then, ye children of Zion, and rejoice in the Lord your God; for He hath given you the former rain moderately, and He will cause to come down for you the rain, the former rain and the latter rain in the first month.

And the floors shall be full of wheat, and the vats shall overflow with wine and oil.

And I will restore to you the years that the locust hath eaten, the cankerworm, and the caterpillar, and the palmer worm, My great army which I sent among you.

And ye shall eat in plenty, and be satisfied, and praise the name of the Lord, your God, Who hath dealt wondrously with you; and My people shall never be ashamed.

Joel 2:21, 23-26

Have you lost count of the rounds? Is your body so weary you are wondering if you can take another blow? Listen to your Manager. He is urging you to go on.

Looking unto Jesus the author and finisher of our faith; Who for the joy that was set before Him endured the cross, despising the shame, and is set down at the right hand of the throne of God.

For consider Him that endured such contradiction of sinners against Himself, lest ye be wearied and faint in your minds.

Hebrews 12:2-3

You are finding your pace now, your second wind. The end is so close, and your adversary is faltering. Your every blow is finding its mark.

The prize is almost in your grasp.

THE OPENING ROUNDS:
Under New Management

Round 1

Revelation of the Warfare

Most Christians are completely unaware that the Body of Christ is in a battle. We sit in our churches and hear about love and blessings, but are totally unprepared for warfare. We are in the same spiritual condition that we are in the natural—flabby and out of shape! How many Christians could go into a fifteen-round fight? Most of us wouldn't last half a round!

Many Christians are not aware that the fight begins at the cross. We stepped into a "boxing ring" when we surrendered our lives to Jesus and became born again. Some people wonder why they feel so beat up, why they are bruised, bloodied, and even knocked out for the count by the devices of the enemy. We do not know our main opponents—the flesh, the world and the devil.

Our biggest battle takes place inside of us, between our spirit and our flesh natures. God first created man a spirit-being in His own image. Then He created a body for this spirit-being from the dust of the earth and called him Adam. He fashioned Eve out of Adam's body and soul.

Essentially, God made man out of Himself, then wrapped him in earth. This house of earth for the new spirit-being could allow him to exist in the material realm and do the work of God. That is the only reason God made us: to be channels of His

Spirit to accomplish His purposes, and because He made us in
His own image, He loves us.

When Eve listened to the serpent and Adam listened to Eve,
they disobeyed God and something terrible happened to them.
God came looking for them in the cool of the evening as He always did, but this time they had hidden themselves. God knew
they had eaten the fruit of the forbidden tree—their actions
betrayed them. For the first time since their creation, Adam and
Eve realized they were naked (Genesis 3:7-8).

What was man covered with before the fall? Adam and Eve
were covered with the glory of God.

When Jesus was raised from the dead, what was He covered
with? His linen grave clothes? No, He left those in the tomb
(Luke 24:12). He was covered with His glory. Although Jesus
was seen at various times by more than five hundred people between His resurrection and ascension (1 Corinthians 15:6),
none of them saw Him naked or in natural clothes—He was
covered with the glory of God.

The glory of God was the covering that Adam and Eve
lost when they sinned. Their original sin upset God's naturally ordained order of government within man, and it set up the
on-going "boxing match" within man and in his fallen world.
Heaven was not made for these unregenerated bodies that we
walk around in on earth. Scripture makes it very plain that the
spirit goes to Heaven, not the flesh. Yet flesh does not want to
die. The flesh and the carnal nature that goes with it must go to
the cross. All flesh eventually will go to the grave (Hebrews
9:27; 1 Corinthians 15:22), except those still alive when Jesus
returns. Their bodies will be instantly transformed (1 Corinthians 15:52).

Because of the strong pull of the flesh (Galatians 5:17, the
flesh lusteth against the spirit), we also try to make war in the
flesh, although the Bible says that our enemies are not flesh and
blood, but spirit (Ephesians 6:12). When we war in the flesh

against flesh and blood controlled by the enemy, we lose. Flesh can never beat demons or satan.

Our first priority is the war against our own flesh. The spirit within man is the real person living in a body of flesh. The spirit-man must fight to control the flesh encasing him. Christian leaders who have fallen in recent years were beaten because they did not fight their own flesh. They lost the bout and went down for the count.

There are five steps by which leadership falls:

1. **Ambition**—If you become ambitious to attain something God never intended for you to attain, then you have taken the first step downward toward defeat. The unholy desire to be number one, to have the biggest church or television audience, to get the most attention and have the most followers, has been and will continue to be the driving force for many Christian leaders. It is always the beginning of the end.

2. **Pride**—Pride gets involved because flesh is always proud. Pride is worthless and good for nothing. If you took it to a pawn shop, they would throw you out. It weighs us down, yet we take it everywhere we go. Have you ever known people with too much ambition? That is pride. It keeps you out of the anointing and always precedes a fall.

3. **Rebellion against authority**—When pride develops, there follows an attitude that no one else can tell you what to do. Rebellion is the "spirit of Absalom," a kind of leprosy or cancer that cripples and destroys the members of the Body of Christ. In the Bible, leprosy always symbolizes rebellion, which is as the sin of witchcraft (Numbers 12:1-15).

4. **Deception**—Rebellion puts you in a position to be easily deceived in two ways. Scripture says that evil men

and imposters go about "deceiving and being deceived"
(2 Timothy 3:13). If you only listen to people who agree
with you and get rid of those who do not agree—beware!
Deception leads to perversion.

5. **Perversion**—Once you are deceived, it is easy for the
devil to stir up something you feel you must fight over to
defend yourself and your position, or you will attack
someone who is different because you feel threatened.
That's what we see in the Body of Christ when any minister becomes a power unto himself.

Some ministers get to the place where they think they are
called to control the spiritual lives of the people. But that's not
enough—they usually want to control their physical lives as
well; and after that, they demand total submission: first in spirit,
then in body. Jim Jones and the Guyana tragedy of the seventies
perfectly illustrates how satan can win when Christians yield to
the flesh. The lust for total power is in every human heart and
the only antidote is to submit to an authority who is under
authority. All of us should be under authority (management).

In the natural boxing ring, some boxers develop special tactics and techniques. One of these is the "feint," a swift swing or
punch with one fist designed to distract the opponent from the
real knockout punch coming from the other unnoticed fist.

The Apostle Paul wrote to the church at Corinth, *we are not
ignorant of his* (satan's) *devices* (2 Corinthians 2:11). I wish
more of us in the Kingdom could say that with honesty, but the
truth is, we keep falling for the same con game (that sin that
doth so easily beset us time and time again—Hebrews 12:1).

Satan has special forces (satanic commandos) specially
trained and anointed to seduce the ministers of God. Their tactics include pornographic literature, videos, movies and other
means of sexual enticements. I can't overemphasize the importance of this truth—the ultimate goal of satan is to destroy the
testimony of the Church, the message and the minister.

When Sister Anne and I first started Rock Church in Virginia Beach, Virginia, there was a woman that used to call me late at night. She would tell me how lonely she felt and how mistreated and misunderstood she was. She had a story that would make anyone want to help her. One night we were asleep and the phone rang. I picked up the phone and it was this same lady. My wife asked me who it was, and when I told her, she took the phone out of my hand and personally told the lady to stop calling our home; if she needed help, come to the church and she would counsel her personally. She never called the house again, nor did she come for counseling.

One day I was on "The 700 Club" answering the phones during a telethon when the lady next to me said there was someone on her phone who wanted to speak with me. It was the same woman. She said she wanted me to come to her house to see her. She felt that if only I could come and lay hands on her she would be healed. I felt the Holy Spirit begin to speak and I heard myself rebuking the woman. I realized she was part of a trap that satan was setting up for me. As I rebuked the evil spirit operating through her, the woman began to spit out vile curses and laugh almost hysterically. As she laughed, she said, "I didn't get you, but I got your friend, I got your friend." Then she continued to laugh and I hung up.

A few days later a young preacher who pastored a church in our area came to see me. As soon as he sat down, the Holy Spirit spoke to me that he was the one. I told him what had happened with this woman. He began to cry and confessed that he had gone to her house after she had called him many times. She told him that I would be there too. She seduced him. The minister ended up losing his church, but God restored him. Satan has prepared a seducing woman or man for every minister—male and female. We must not be caught unawares.

You can trace nearly every destroyed ministry or broken church to ministers or leaders of the congregation who got involved and entangled in sins of the flesh.

The Bible says that flesh and blood cannot inherit the Kingdom, neither can the natural man receive the things of the Spirit. Christian leaders fall because there are parts of their old natures that have never been dealt with. They tried to build the Kingdom of God with flesh and blood, and it cannot be done.

Now this I say, brethren, that flesh and blood cannot inherit the kingdom of God; neither doth corruption inherit incorruption.

1 Corinthians 15:50

We do not hear God with our natural ears, nor do we understand the things of God with our natural minds. The Apostle Paul wrote:

Now we have received, not the spirit of the world, but the spirit which is of God; that we might know the things that are freely given to us of God.

Which things also we speak, not in the words which man's wisdom teacheth, but which the Holy Ghost teacheth; comparing spiritual things with spiritual.

But the natural man receiveth not the things of the Spirit of God: for they are foolishness unto him: neither can he know them, because they are spiritually discerned.

1 Corinthians 2:12-14

God Speaks to the Spirits of Men

From the fall of Adam and Eve to the coming of the Holy Spirit on the Day of Pentecost, all that mankind possessed were the *senses of the flesh.* God could not speak to their inner man, so He had to appear Himself, give dreams and visions, or send angels. The Holy Spirit was given to the children of God after Jesus ascended to Heaven to restore our "spiritual nervous systems."

By His life on earth, Jesus was saying, "Look at Me. This is the way you should be, and this is the way you should live—in complete obedience to the Father." You cannot do this unless you "crucify" the flesh and bring it to "death," so that the spirit-man within you is the ruler of the soul and body.

The Lord recently showed me something about the dead past we like to drag around with us. When the Apostle Paul wrote about the "old man" in Romans 6:6, Ephesians 4:22 and Colossians 3:9, he was describing the flesh nature that we thought was our *real* life until we were born again. That flesh is *dead*, because it does not have the life of God in it.

The first step in our personal spiritual boxing match with our flesh is to understand that we must leave our past behind now that we have met the living God.

Saul of Tarsus had Christians arrested, tortured and put to death (Acts 22:5). Yet, in his later life as the blood-washed Apostle Paul, he was able to say that he was innocent of the blood of all men (Acts 20:26). How could he say that? After he met Jesus on the road to Damascus, he literally became a new man. Obviously, however, he had to let go of the "old man," the flesh, which was a process (Philippians 2:12). Paul had a clear understanding of being a new man.

Paul apparently struggled for some time to let go of the flesh, just as we do. He wrote that the things he wanted to do, he did not, and the things he did not want to do—he did (Romans 7:15). The first spiritual fight for a Christian is to put the past behind him, bury the dead, and receive the resurrection power of Christ in his life (Philippians 3:10).

In practical terms, this means we must guard our thoughts if we want to win the fight with the past. God does not want us to meditate on the evil and corruption of our past. He wants us to think on those things that are true, honest and lovely (Philippians 4:8).

In the beginning of my Christian life, all I did was visit various churches and share my testimony about what a dirty drug addict I had been, along with the bad things I had done. I told them about my hate, resentment and bitterness.

Then I went to Bible school, and hated it. Bible school confined me—it tried to break me, mold me, change me, discipline me. I felt like I was back in jail. I wanted to do as I pleased. I felt almost superior to my teachers. I still had a rebellious attitude and hated the authority I found myself under. I began to feel God had left me because I seemed to have lost my fervor for Him, so I decided to leave the school.

Before I left, I received a phone call from Anne. We had broken our engagement, but she felt led to call and share with me what God had spoken to her. She told me that God would let me die if I returned to New York City. She said God told her that I was to call Reverend David Minor. Afterwards, I called him and as soon as I told him, "This is John Gimenez," he immediately began to speak in other tongues and prophesy. Through Brother Minor, the Lord said I was to go to his home and there He would meet me in a special way.

Several days later, while in the room at his home, I received a vision from the Lord. He showed me a dirty old cot with prison bars in front of it stretching from the mud to the heavens, and I was lying on the cot with a long dirty beard (in the natural, I have never had a beard). I had long hair, and lice were crawling all over me. Next to me was lying a corrupt dead body.

I said, "Lord, why have You forsaken me?"

He said, "I have never forsaken you. You are the one who has forsaken Me."

Then He showed me that I had been carrying a dead body around with me, testifying to everyone that I was a "dirty" this and a "rotten" that. I had never let go of the past—the old man—nor had I walked in the newness of life that was mine by right once I was born again.

Even after you get saved, there are "undercover agents" still present. Some are demonic influences, some are "imaginations," some are certain attitudes and behaviors. We must fight through spiritual warfare to get rid of whatever lingers there in the flesh. This is the only way to begin living and acting like the new person we are, rather than like the old person we were.

Who or what are some of the enemies that we must learn to fight? Habits can be enemies dwelling in the flesh. Did you ever have a habit you wished God would take away? The funny thing is that whenever you say, "God, take this away from me," God will answer, "You give it up."

Paul said we have to put off the "old man" and put on the new, once we are born again. The human spirit is made new through the blood of Jesus, but the things of the soul and body have to be laid down one by one.

This is the process Jesus described when He said, *If any man will come after Me, let him deny himself, and take up his cross daily, and follow Me* (Luke 9:23). We must choose to lay down the things of the flesh and the old man so our outer man will be consistent with the inner man. The Bible calls this "conforming to the image of Jesus."

> *For whom He did foreknow, He also did predestinate to be conformed to the image of His Son, that He might be the Firstborn among many brethren.*
>
> Romans 8:29

> *And be not conformed to this world: but be ye transformed by the renewing of your mind, that ye may prove what is that good, and acceptable, and perfect, will of God.*
>
> Romans 12:2

The Church as a whole has not let go of the dead past. We need to have an examination of the Body. New medical technology is available that will scan your brain and nervous system. Technicians can print out on paper the types and characteristics of disorders or sicknesses they find in the body so that they can be recognized and dealt with.

I believe the Holy Spirit is doing this now for the Body of Christ. He is exposing all of the sicknesses. Because individual Christians and entire churches are trying to mix flesh with spirit, the enemy can use even good, well-meaning people to shut down the move of the Spirit of God in the nations.

To deal with the things of our time, the Church must move out of her "comfort zone," out of thinking that God's love means never being corrected. That idea stems from modern "child-rearing" methods that are not biblical. We are in warfare!

We must begin to believe the whole Bible, and relearn the part where God says He loves you because He chastises you (Hebrews 12:6-11).

The Bible says that if God does not correct you, you are illegitimate. Without correction, you will not let go of the dead past. Without correction and adjustment in the Church, God's people will never experience the unity needed in our generation.

One of the biggest problems hindering Christians today is their disunity. The flesh keeps us from coming into unity as a Body. This is a serious problem because *without unity* there can be *no blessings, no increase, and no manifested glory of God*!

Soldiers, trying to fight an enemy without being "in one accord," will never win the battle. And fighters who enter the boxing ring and don't fight to win had better get used to losing.

Round 2

The Need for Unity in the Church

The Church of the nineties has received great teachings from anointed evangelists, pastors, and teachers, even from prophets and apostles. However, I know in my spirit the greatest need in all of Christendom is the teaching, preaching and demonstration of the unity of the Body of Christ.

We are in a real fight. The problem is, we are fighting the wrong opponent. We are fighting flesh and blood. We are fighting each other.

I believe God is sternly warning us with a loud voice: *the Church of Jesus Christ must be one!* God has always wanted His people to live and walk in unity—just as He and His Son are one.

Behold, how good and how pleasant it is for brethren to dwell together in unity!

It is like the precious ointment upon the head, that ran down upon the beard, even Aaron's beard: that went down to the skirts of his garments;

As the dew of Hermon, and as the dew that descended upon the mountains of Zion: for there the Lord commanded the blessing, even life for evermore.

Psalm 133:1-3

Somehow, it is hard for us to grasp the concept that we are one Family—the House of God. Jesus said that if a house is divided against itself, it cannot stand (Matthew 12:25). Jesus is all-powerful, but if the Church remains divided, scattered and out of unity, a toothless devil can defeat us.

Amos said, "Can two walk together except they be agreed?" (Amos 3:3)

When Jesus was told His mother and brothers were at the door looking for Him, He said, "My mother and brothers are those who do the will of My Father" (Mark 3:34-35). Born again brothers and sisters in the Lord have a stronger tie than natural blood.

Some professing Christians love the Lord, but according to John the Apostle, the love of God isn't in them because they do not love their brothers (1 John 4:20). Many of these believers struggle to obey God's commandment to love one another because of man-made traditions they have been taught by misled church leaders and Bible teachers who scatter rather than gather the flock (Matthew 12:30-31).

Jesus named only *one thing* that would show the world that we were of God—He said, "By this shall all men know that ye are My disciples, if ye have love one to another" (John 13:35).

If the world cannot see the brethren loving one another, why should they believe that God exists or that He loves them? We are giving the Lord a bad name in the world with our divisions and lack of unity. Many people ask, "If you really believe in Christ, why are you always fighting one another? You are a bunch of hypocrites."

Jesus said we cannot effectively pray if we have something against a brother or a brother against us. He said our sacrifices, or offerings, would do no good (Matthew 5:23-24).

To those who are sure the Church is going to get caught up "out of this sinful world" any day, I have news for you! It is impossible for the Church to be raptured today, or tomorrow!

Jesus is not coming for a Bride full of spots and blemishes (2 Peter 2:13).

A Church divided cannot preach the gospel of the Kingdom to the whole world, and Jesus said the end would come *after* that is done (Matthew 24:14).

Jesus said, *I pray that they may be one as We are one* (John 17:21). He wasn't praying that we would have unity of mind and action in certain causes, such as political ideas, but unity of heart.

One person said, "I can join with you in politics, because I believe we have to get this country straightened out. But I can't get together with you in a prayer meeting. You guys pray too loud!"

Another said, "We can unite and pray in Washington for our nation, but I can't take Communion with you. Our doctrines are different."

We are operating in limited unions. We unite for short periods for activist reasons, not for unity in relationship. Since we have been born into the same family, we need to begin to act like it. The Body of Christ is not the Baptist body, the Roman Catholic body, the Lutheran body or the Pentecostal body. It is one family—in spite of all the different doctrines—not because of them. We are in unity for one reason: Jesus Christ. The problem is that we do not act, live or work in unity. We are a "house divided."

Jesus is our peace, our bond of unity and harmony (Ephesians 2:14). He made one in Himself of all races, nations, classes and genders who have received Him. He broke down and destroyed the hostile dividing wall between us.

To the devil's delight, the Church has managed to erect new walls of partition built from different beliefs and different interpretations of the Word. Jesus made everyone equal in Him, but we have made that of no effect through our doctrines and traditions.

Some years ago, I talked to an official of the state church of Germany about our desire to see the Body of Christ come together in unity. He said, "Well, you Americans are so flamboyant, so demonstrative, and so emotional. We like things the way they are here in Germany." The nation was divided by the Berlin Wall at that time.

That mentality only builds new walls of separation, undoing what Jesus did on the cross. Others say, "Leave us alone. We like our cliques, our divisions, our own group. We do not want to mingle."

I would like to ask them, "What are you going to do in Heaven? There are not going to be black and white sections, Hispanic and German sections, male and female sections. We are all going to be together as one!"

The spirit of jealousy and competition erects walls. This is the spirit that caused Joseph's brothers to sell him into slavery (Genesis 37:4, 8, 11), and moved David's brothers to jeer at him just before he went out to slay the giant (1 Samuel 17:28). This same spirit is still in operation, moving through the Church today.

The Spirit of Division Separates The Body

When the spirit of jealousy joins with the spirit of greed in an individual or a group, it creates a spirit of division. This attitude caused Abraham and Lot to separate.

In Genesis 13:6-11, the workers for both men were fighting over the sheep. Today, when some pastors or churches lose sheep to another, they begin to spread the rumor that the other guy is "preaching false doctrine." Where does greed come into all this?

When you lose sheep, you lose "wool," symbolic of tithes and offerings. Fearing they'll lose some tithe and offering income, some pastors actually tell their people not to go hear so-and-so, because he is "preaching heresies" when they have never heard the other minister and don't even know what he preaches! A spirit of greed has moved them to gossip and give a false witness.

Another spirit that prevents unity is complacency. A guest minister at Rock Church once said there are three kinds of Christians:

1. The kind who make things happen.

2. The kind who watch things happen and say, "That's nice. I see it. Those people are going to do this thing," but they do not get involved.

3. The kind who wonder, "What happened?" and do not even know what is going on—they are not concerned.

I would add a fourth category: Those who think that without them the job is not going to get done. This type of Christian is proud of his own importance. The spirit of pride is a Christian's most deadly enemy.

The enemy is hard at work creating dissension. Look at the fighting between Catholics and Protestants in Ireland. There are those in this country who would love to see the same religious bigotry going on here. Others would like to see war between the races.

The members of the Body of Christ are not supposed to fight each other, but love one another. If we experienced a revival that brought unity, Christians would not permit division to start. Immediately there would be ambassadors of unity going straight to the problem to deal with it.

For there to be unity in the Body of Christ, there must first be unity in the home between husband and wife, and between parents and children. To have unity between races and nations, there must be unity in the Church. As the Church goes, so goes the world. We are to be salt and light.

God chose the Church before the foundation of the world (Ephesians 1:4). Jesus loved the Church so much that He freely gave His life for it (Ephesians 5:25). That is why I am staggered by some of the actions of men and women who preach the Gospel and yet dare violate the love of Jesus. We should do nothing to hurt the Church, but everything to build her up!

Some parachurch ministries damage the local church by telling their listeners, "Send me your tithes." At the same time, some local churches preach against parachurch ministries.

Jesus suffered the agony of the trial and crucifixion for the joy set before Him. He endured the pain, the humiliation, the separation from His Father, and death itself on the cross because He could see His joy, the Church, shining out in beauty and glory because of the agony He was suffering (Hebrews 12:2).

Jesus is personally committed to building His Church. He gave His life for the Church. He said the gates of hell will not prevail against it. He said that upon the rock of belief in Him would He build His Church (Matthew 16:18). Somehow, we forget that *it is His Church*, thinking that some parts of it are ours. We forget Who suffered and gave His life for the Church. Most of us can barely let go of our tithes for it, let alone our lives.

Jesus' commitment stands for something. When He says a thing, it happens. When He promises something, you can "take it to the bank." If every television and radio station in the world stopped carrying Christian programming, and if each publication, book, and Bible was taken away, Jesus would still build His Church.

Russia and China have tried to kill the Church in the modern age. Idi Amin tried to snuff it out in his country, and stronger rulers have tried in the past and failed—even though they thought they held total power over their nations and people. They forgot about the all-powerful God and His Son, the King of kings.

The Roman Empire tried, but which kingdom fell—the Empire or the Church? In our day, which was the most powerful nation? Which "nation" outlived politics, repression and competing "philosophies"— the Soviet Union or the Church? Did Idi Amin triumph or the Church? I've got news for you—it's in the Book: the same thing will happen to China or any other nation that tries to stop, hinder or destroy the Church of Jesus Christ.

We are told that "all things" are ours (1 Corinthians 3:21-23). The Apostle John declared that overcomers will sit with Jesus on His throne (Revelation 3:21). We are going to rule and reign with Him. We are promised that if we share His sufferings, we will share His riches and glory (Romans 8:17).

The Church is to be the light of the world. When her operations are stopped, from the inside or outside, there is real trouble (Matthew 5:14). The darkness of the devil moves in when the Church moves out or abdicates its place as the light.

When Jesus said "I will build My Church" in Matthew 16:18, He meant just that: *HE* is going to build it the way *HE* wants it, no matter how long it takes.

Denominations and movements of the past have tried to build the Church, and they have all contributed something. However, when any of them stepped out of line with Jesus' blueprint for them, or when they sat down on what they had built and refused to move on, He stopped providing materials.

He is saying, "I'm not going to help you build your kingdom. You must help Me build Mine. All of you will fail until you decide to do it My way."

The Church Is Not an Afterthought

The Church is a many-membered body, carefully built by Jesus Himself to be His Bride. When you go to a well-planned wedding, everything is put together to achieve a harmonious event. When the bride comes down the aisle, every person turns and smiles, because she is beautiful and radiant. It is a love

scene. That is what Jesus is coming for: a Bride adorned with
His glory.

The Church was in the heart of God from the beginning. The
late Dr. Paul E. Billheimer wrote something in his book, *Destined for the Throne*, that is so true:

> The human race was created in the image and like-
> ness of God for one purpose: to provide an eternal com-
> panion for the Son of God.
>
> God did not create the human race that it might
> devour and destroy itself with hatred and war. He
> created the human race so that He would have a com-
> panion for His Son, Jesus Christ.
>
> After the fall of man, God promised redemption, and
> Israel was born and nurtured in order to bring the Mes-
> siah. That is why God chose Israel, so that from them,
> He could bring forth the Messiah. The Messiah came for
> one intent: to give birth to His Church, to obtain His
> Bride, the called-out Body of the Redeemed. Mankind
> turned out to be the central object, the goal, not only of
> land and history but of all that God has been doing in all
> realms from all eternity. Thus the universe and all there-
> in from the beginning has been cooperating with God to
> select and train His Church for the eternal companion of
> Jesus, the inheritor of all things.

The Church is the inheritor of all things. The Church is the
apple of God's eye. It is the reason God brought life on this
planet and instituted the human race. His sole, absolute purpose
is to bring forth, out of all humanity, a Bride for His Son.

The Words of God are the very essence of Jesus. John wrote
that Jesus is the Word of God (John 1:1). When Jesus said, "I
will build My Church," He was speaking to the Father, making
a promise to fulfill the Father's purpose. Also, He was speaking

for God, for the powers of the universe. He was the sum total of those powers.

The word *build* suggests a long, slow, drawn-out process. Paul tells us in Ephesians 2:20 that the Church is built on the foundation of the apostles and prophets and that Jesus Himself is the Cornerstone. So Jesus first had to come to earth and defeat the works of satan before He could achieve His goal of building the Church.

It takes time to build a large edifice. One must lay the foundations and have the right mixture of materials to build with.

God has the master plan well in hand. He has a time schedule known only to Him (Matthew 24:36). He is the Architect of the universe, and He knows what it will take to finish His building. He knows every small "ingredient" (person) it will take to complete it.

Jesus purchased His Bride with His own blood (Acts 20:28; 1 Peter 1:18-19). Paul wrote that husbands should love their wives as Christ loves the Church and gave Himself for it (Ephesians 5:25). How many husbands today would be willing to purchase their brides with their own blood?! Jesus loved the Church enough to give Himself for it. From the beginning of time, and from Genesis to Revelation, that was God's plan.

We are to live for Him, having been chosen for Him. We are to be perfected until we all come to the unity of a perfect man—until we measure up to the stature of the fullness of Christ (Ephesians 4:13). Jesus is not going to come for His Bride until we are one in unity.

We can sit on a mountaintop or hide in a cave; we can write it on the rooftops like the people did in New York; we can even "figure out all the numbers" and set the date of our Lord's return "scientifically," but we will still be wrong!

Jesus will not come until His Bride is ready. He is not going to come back for a bunch of "wimps" or rebels. He is not coming back for a Church whose "parts" hate one another and fight

among themselves. He is coming for a Church in love with Him
and one another, adorned in the beautiful white garments of His
glory, with a perfect veil and crown to match.

The Church can make it without certain members, but the
particular member cannot make it without the Church. There
are people in many churches today saying, "I will not compromise my doctrines for unity." I have news for them: unity is
a doctrine they have already compromised! They are not refus-
ing to compromise their beliefs, they are just choosing which
doctrines to compromise!

Throughout the Pauline epistles, we read "unity, unity, unity
and more unity." Unity in the Body is one of the primary
doctrines in the Word of God. If we are not working toward
that, we are compromising the doctrines of the Word.

I read a comment by one minister who said, "If the ministers
of the Church would get in tune with the desires of Jesus and
make His ministry predominant in their lives instead of their
own desires, we could get this job done."

"If ministers would stop promoting their pet doctrines and
begin to build up and unify the Church of Christ, if they would
put aside their hard-headed, narrow-minded, bigoted, self-
righteous, unteachable, cold-hearted, and indifferent attitudes,
the world would believe that Jesus is the Son of God and many
would be converted."

I believe God wants us to be reconciled to one another. We
were reconciled to Him when Jesus finished His work on the
cross, but we have never become reconciled to one another. We
can send out all the missionaries we want, but the job is not
going to get done until it gets done in and among us.

Anyone who is not working for the unity of the Body is
working in agreement with disunity, in disobedience to the
commandments of Jesus and the desire of the Father. Of course,
there are things I do not understand or agree with in some ministries, but that doesn't mean I am not in unity with them.

Every time I see a wrong in a brother or sister, I wonder, "Do they see something that is wrong with me, too?" If I stay busy, dealing with my own problems (the "beam in my eye"), I will not be focusing on other people's weaknesses (Luke 6:42).

Jesus loves the whole Church and died for it—every race, every social and economic class, every denomination, and every sect that has made Him their Cornerstone.

All of God's promises are for the Universal Church. We cannot receive the promises and blessings without the rest of the Body. For an individual to participate, he must become and remain an active, lively member of the universal body, working for its overall fulfillment.

Round 3

Unity Commands the Blessing

God loves to bless His people, but because of man's rebellious nature, He also made it clear that the opposite of blessing is cursing. God wants to bless; He does not want to curse. He wants to bless so that we can win the battle.

The blessings of the Lord make us rich. They increase, encourage and strengthen us, and God never "attaches" sorrow to them (Proverbs 10:22).

Most of us, being true to human nature, want all the blessings of God, but we also want our own ways. The most important prerequisite to receiving God's blessings is unity in the Body of Christ. It brings an automatic blessing from God when we minister in unity and stay in an attitude of unity with the other brethren (Psalm 133:1-3). I know people say, "You cannot have unity at any cost, or you will miss God." Each group seems to have a different interpretation or explanation of the cost, according to its doctrinal position.

Where do we draw the line? We obviously cannot have unity with groups who do not base salvation on the blood of Jesus, who think we can get into the Kingdom "some other way" (John 10:1). However, as long as brethren are born again through the blood covenant, we can have unity with them.

We must examine the purpose of everything we do to make sure that its ultimate result will bring unity in the Body of Christ. In John 17:21-23, Jesus categorically stated that the only way the world is going to believe that He is the Son of God is by what it sees in the Church. What an awesome responsibility!

The Father gave Jesus His glory and His power for His purpose. Jesus in turn gave that same glory and power to us—that we might fulfill the purpose of the Father which is that we would be "ONE" (John 17:22). This was not just for the disciples of Jesus' day. *He specifically included us* in His "high priestly prayer!"

> *Neither pray I for these alone, but for them also which shall believe on Me through their word;*

> *That they all may be one; as Thou, Father, art in Me, and I in Thee, that they also may be one in us; that the world may believe that Thou has sent Me.*

> *And the glory which Thou gavest Me I have given them; that they may be one, even as we are one:*

> *I in them, and Thou in Me, that they may be made perfect in one; and that the world may know that Thou has sent Me, and hast loved them, as Thou hast loved Me.*

> John 17:20-23

Jesus was saying by implication, "If they do *not* love one another, they hinder My work and stop people from receiving Me. If they disobey My command to love one another, they are saying to the world that I am not Your Son—they are saying by their attitudes that I was not really the Messiah."

If we do not love one another in the Church, we are making a blanket statement to the world that Jesus is not real. The Church will not be blessed as a whole until we love one another. Nor will we walk in God's fullest blessings until we walk in love as individual members of His body.

Love among the brethren lifts up Jesus, and if He is lifted up, He will draw all men to Himself. The context of John 12:32 speaks of the kind of death Jesus would die. He was lifted up on the cross because of love. He dared to love the Father and us enough to endure indescribable suffering. Surely we can pay the price to lift Him up by loving one another as a visible witness to the world that He is real.

What does this truth about unity have to do with spiritual warfare? What does it have to do with becoming a "boxer" in the Kingdom? Everything! Love means preferring your brother above yourself, and love hits the devil where it hurts the most. Love binds us together and preserves us as a supernatural family.

Be kindly affectioned one to another with brotherly love; in honor preferring one another...

Be of the same mind one toward another. Mind not high things, but condescend to (associate with) *men of low estate. Be not wise in your own conceits.*

Romans 12:10, 16

Many verses in the first epistle of John talk about love among the brethren.

Again, a new commandment I write unto you, which thing is true in Him (Jesus) *and in you: because the darkness is past, and the true light now shineth.*

He that saith he is in the light, and hateth his brother, is in darkness even until now.

He that loveth his brother abideth in the light, and there is none occasion of stumbling in him.

But he that hateth his brother is in darkness, and walketh in darkness, and knoweth not whither he goeth, because that darkness hath blinded his eyes.

1 John 2:8-11

For this is the message that ye heard from the beginning, that we should love one another...

And this is His commandment, That we should believe on the name of His Son Jesus Christ, and love one another, as He gave us commandment.

1 John 3:11, 23

Beloved, let us love one another: for love is of God; and everyone that loveth is born of God, and knoweth God.

He that loveth not knoweth not God; for God is love...

Beloved, if God so loved us (as to send His Son to die for us), *we ought also to love one another...*

We love Him because He first loved us.

If a man say, I love God, and hateth his brother, he is a liar: for he that loveth not his brother whom he hath seen, how can he love God whom he hath not seen?

1 John 4:7-8, 11, 19, 20

When we are the center of attention, we are in trouble. Even the great prophet Elijah thought he was the only one God had left—when in reality there were 7,000 others in Israel who had not bowed the knee to Baal (1 Kings 19:18). Unfortunately, Elijah's attitude is prevalent today. Many preachers feel they are "the only ones" with the whole truth.

The Body is Many, Not Just One

Woe to any minister or Christian who brings division to the Bride of Christ! Woe to those who act against unity, not for it!

Praise God there are many great men in Christendom today who have never lost sight of the fact that they are only one particular part of the entire Body of Christ. The spirits and attitudes of these men are focused on bringing unity in the Church.

The Apostle Paul made it very clear that the Church is an organism—not an organization:

For I say, through the grace given unto me, to every man that is among you, not to think of himself more highly than he ought to think; but to think soberly, according as God hath dealt to every man the measure of faith.

For as we have many members in one body, and all members have not the same office:

So we, being many, are one body in Christ, and every one members one of another.

Romans 12:3-5

Paul went on to list some of the gifts that God has given various members of the Body to help put us together and teach us to operate in the will of the Holy Spirit. As we obey God's Word and the leading of the Holy Spirit, we will be made one, and the Church will be able to spread the gospel of the Kingdom to every nation and tongue.

In Ephesians, Paul listed the ministry gifts that Jesus gave to the Body at large to perfect the saints and equip them for ministry:

And He gave some, apostles; and some, prophets; and some, evangelists; and some, pastors and teachers;

For the perfecting of the saints, for the work of the ministry, for the edifying of the body of Christ;

Till we all come in the unity of the faith, and of the knowledge of the Son of God, unto a perfect man, unto the measure of the stature of the fulness of Christ:

That we henceforth be no more children, tossed to and fro, and carried about with every wind of doctrine, by the sleight of men, and cunning craftiness, whereby they lie in wait to deceive;

But speaking the truth in love, may grow up into Him in all things, which is the head, even Christ:

From whom the whole body fitly joined together and compacted by that which every joint supplieth, according to the effectual working in the measure of every part, maketh increase of the body unto the edifying of itself in love.

Ephesians 4:11-16

Unity indicates spiritual maturity. God's people in the twentieth century are too much like the Corinthian church of Paul's day, in need of milk when the people ought themselves to be teaching (1 Corinthians 3:1). The "modern" Church is full of carnality with its "immature," childish behavior. The author of Hebrews knew this when he wrote:

For when for the time ye ought to be teachers, ye have need that one teach you again which be the first principles of the oracles of God; and are become such as have need of milk, and not of strong meat.

For everyone that useth milk is unskilful in the word of righteousness: for he is a babe.

But strong meat belongeth to them that are of full age, even those who by reason of use have their senses exercised to discern both good and evil.

Hebrews 5:12-14

Loving the brethren and being committed to unity demands Christians "of full age," those who have had "their senses exercised to discern both good and evil." Division and dissension among the brethren is evil; unity among the brethren is good. Showing the world that Jesus is real because we love one another requires mature spiritual natures.

Christians today are fighting unity under the guise of "not being carried away by every wind of doctrine." By setting themselves apart, they are being "carried away" by their own doctrines—in direct disobedience to the letter and spirit of God's Word. The Pharisees also set aside the Word of God for their own traditional teachings in Jesus' day, and became the targets of Jesus' wrath for their actions (Matthew 15:3-6).

Sadly enough, it is not the weak ones who get puffed up and bring division, but rather the strong—but spiritually childish—ones. When you see men and women of God operating in a great anointing and being used in a tremendous way, pray for them. They are prime targets for the devil's deceptive attack with pride.

If they come tumbling down, they usually bring a lot of people with them. The pride of man brings division in the Body. When a minister begins to preach division, it draws the sheep to an individual, not to Jesus.

Do you remember the appalling story of the late Jim Jones in Guyana? He began as a little preacher. Then the day came when he got so big in his own eyes that the Bible was beneath him. He actually took it and flung it on the floor, stepped on it, and said he did not need it anymore. He thought he was above it.

The Bible says that *God* adds to the Church daily, *not man* (Acts 2:47). When you walk in love and unity with the brethren, God's blessings are upon you. God's blessings bring increase in all areas of your life. If you are a minister preaching unity, the Lord will increase your church.

Unity Brings the Blessing of Increase

God will send sheep and lambs to a church that lifts Him up because the spirit of unity in Christ is there, and He knows it is safe for the sheep. Secondly, He will also bless the obedient pastor by multiplying disciples (disciplined ones) in his ministry.

And He gives you warriors (intercessors). The Word of God says "five of you shall chase an hundred, and an hundred of you shall put ten thousand to flight" (Leviticus 26:8).

There is a spiritual progression that goes along with the blessings of God toward those who keep His commandment to be one. Instead of one plus one is two, two plus two is four, or even one times five is five, blessings will increase geometrically. Five will outdo a hundred, and a hundred will put ten thousand to flight.

With that principle, it won't take many people preaching unity to turn the whole world upside down for Jesus. It only took one hundred and twenty in the upper room on the Day of Pentecost to turn their world upside down because they were in one accord (Acts 1:15; 2:1).

Unity will save the home, the nation and the Church! Unity is the guarantee that Jesus will come back for an integrated Bride. I know brethren who hate one another. When you hear each of them preach, you marvel at the anointing and the revelation of the Word of God, yet they hate one another.

We need ministers who will preach and teach unity, but more importantly, will demonstrate it among themselves. There are too few ambassadors of unity in Christendom. There are no mature representatives sent by the Church when there are separations, a lack of communication, or problems among the brethren.

Until we change, Jesus cannot come back. To see revival in our time (and I believe we will), we must get together in love and begin to live and minister in the spiritual maturity Paul wrote about. Unity will bring greater blessings than we can imagine. Paul spoke of this when he wrote to the church at Rome:

And I am sure that, when I come unto you, I shall come in the fulness of the blessing of the gospel of Christ.

Romans 15:29

For the earth which drinketh in the rain that cometh oft upon it, and bringeth forth herbs meet for them by whom it is dressed, receiveth blessing from God:

But that which beareth thorns and briers is rejected, and is nigh unto cursing; whose end is to be burned.

Hebrews 6:7-8

Perhaps the strongest connection made between unity and blessings is found in 1 Peter 3:8-9:

Finally, be ye all of one mind (be in unity, be in one accord), *having compassion one of another, love as brethren, be pitiful* (compassionate), *be courteous:*

Not rendering evil for evil, or railing for railing, but contrariwise, blessing, knowing that ye are called (commanded) *to this, that ye should inherit a blessing.*

We can only be blessed if we are one. Unity brings blessings, and unity brings the glory of the Lord.

Round 4

Unity Brings the Glory of God

Every minister is called to preach on a certain aspect of the Gospel. Most ministers do their best to present "the whole counsel of God" in their ministries, but when God lays a strong burden for a particular area or need, that burden will often shape or dominate that ministry for years, or a lifetime. At some point, the Lord may change their emphasis and move them on to something else. During this time period, when a particular facet of the Christian life is laid on the minister's heart, nearly everything he preaches will be developed around it. The Lord has given me a great burden for the reconciliation of the Church and the bringing of unity among the brethren. Whatever text I take, that theme comes out of it!

Ministers go over and over the same subject when it is their calling or assignment at that time and people learn best by repetition. The literal meaning of the Greek word for *meditate* is to chew on something like a cow does her cud. Take it in, bring it up, chew on it, swallow it, bring it up again, chew on it, until whatever you have taken in is digestible (understood).

Nutritionists note that many physical problems come from not chewing food properly to make it more digestible. I believe many Christians do not properly digest what they hear for the same reason. They just don't take the time needed to chew on it, to "meditate" God's Word.

Some months ago, I began to teach about the man with palsy who was healed (Mark 2:1-12). Jesus found this sick person with need in the middle of a big crowd of healthy people who had flocked to hear Him. The Lord showed me that the Church is sick with spiritual palsy.

Palsy is an illness that causes the limbs and the head to shake. Because of this shaking, a person cannot function properly and has little strength; their limbs may not move together in a coordinated motion as they should. With one arm flailing around one way, and the other trying to grasp something, it takes a long time to accomplish a purpose, if it gets done at all. If it's not in unity as God ordained it to be, it is out of control.

When those men began to take out a section of the roof to lower their friend to Jesus, imagine the pandemonium that broke out. The roof was literally and figuratively the covering of man. Man put that roof there to protect himself from the rain, the wind, and sun. But man's covering meant nothing to the friends of the man on that cot. He must have been trembling with his sickness, but was so intent on getting to Jesus that he didn't care what people thought or how much commotion he stirred up. The people below must have thought he was crazy, certainly out of order, and probably "just trying to attract attention."

He was looking from face to face for the Messiah, and probably wondering, "Where is this Jesus of Nazareth? What will He look like? How tall is He? Is it really true? Can He really heal me and make me whole?"

Suddenly, he came face to face with the Son of God, the promised Messiah, the Son of David, the Everlasting One, the Righteous Branch, the Way, the Truth, and the Life. He looked into the eternal face of God mirrored in the eyes of Jesus. Jesus said, "Thy sins be forgiven." This is always the first thing that has to happen in a healing.

No revival ever comes without a wave of repentance and prayer for renewal first. If the Church of the Lord Jesus Christ is ever going to be the Church of Glory and turn the world around, we must humble ourselves and repent, beginning with the top leaders.

Repentance in the local church must begin with the pastor. Pastors and leaders around the world must get on their knees and repent for not obeying the commandments of God, including His outright command that we love one another in unity.

Church leaders must begin loving one another, forgiving one another, preferring one another. When a spiritual move begins at the top, it becomes like rain from Heaven, filtering down to touch leadership first and then the people. The people are ready! If the leaders would humble themselves, the "people outside" would be "tearing off the roof" of man-made coverings that keep the rain of glory from falling.

After the healing of the palsied man, there were some who questioned what happened. There will always be people who question the things of God—even Christian "questioners." This kind of negativity didn't alter the fact that someone repented and was healed. That man had been healed and he knew it, and so did the crowd around him! This must happen in the Church! There are no options. The Word of God gives no other way for the Church to prepare for the return of the Bridegroom. Those who won't encourage this healing of the Body are false prophets, blind leaders of the blind (Matthew 15:14). Unity brings the glory. Leaders who do not move into unity keep the glory of Jesus from the Church and the world.

God intended the Church to be well and not be sick. It is "shaking" with a lot of activities and programs, but it is not moving in one direction—and a body not moving in one direction will soon be torn apart.

We are not "in one accord!" People don't like to hear this because they want to stay the way they are. People who like sicknesses are called hypochondriacs. They talk about "their" latest sickness, calling their friends to talk about all the symptoms, hoping to draw sympathy. This type of person can identify with an illness and feel possessive about it. He can begin to talk about it as "my sickness." (If you do this kind of thing, you certainly will keep it, for you have claimed it as your own.)

God does not want us to be sick, and He certainly does not want the Church of Jesus Christ to be sick. God wants to take sickness away from us and the Church. He wants His Body to be healthy, active and strong.

How can we know if we are spiritually sick? We are spiritually sick if we feel antagonistic, bitter or jealous toward other Christians, or if we do not like to go to church, pray or read the Bible.

To be healed, we must recognize that we are sick, and we must want help. The Church is sick and does not know it. Its individual members are not "discerning the Body." The Bible says that in the early days of the Church there were many sick among the the believers because they did not discern the Body (1 Corinthians 11:29). That means they did not have a complete knowledge or understanding of the Body of Christ. Jesus Christ is the Head, not us. We want to act like the head, not the big toe or thumb or some uncomely part (1 Corinthians 12:24).

We Need People Who Care

We live in a world of hungry, naked, sick people, a world where violence is increasing with drugs, murder, abortion, rape and pornography. All of these things are designed to destroy the human race. Someone must begin to care and it should be the Church, those who are called the "light" and "salt" of the world. Jesus said if salt loses its essence, its only remaining use is to be thrown out and walked on (Matthew 5:13). Judging by the public disrespect for the Church today, we have lost our "saltiness," our ability to "flavor" society with righteousness.

Sometimes I am accused of being controversial. No, I just care. I care about the condition of this nation and my community. I care about the young people dying from substance addictions and the increasing rates of violence and unwed mothers. I care about the Church! It should be offering hope as an ark of safety to these people—but it's not.

Anne and I travel everywhere telling people, "Come on, let's get together. Let's love one another! Let the Presbyterians, Methodists, Baptists, Independents, Assemblies of God, Lutherans, and all the others say with one voice: There is one Lord, one Spirit, one Church, and one Body" (Ephesians 4:4).

The four men who lowered the crippled man through the roof cared enough to do something for their friend who could not help himself. They took him to the place of healing and tore off the roof to get him to the One who could heal. They were like the hundred and twenty on the Day of Pentecost who were determined not to leave until they achieved their desired end.

God needs people today who refuse to let go until His purpose is accomplished. He needs people to "stay in the ring" until the spirit of division in the Body is given a knock out blow!

There is a place of healing today for all who are sick in body, mind or heart. There is Someone with the right medication. You simply have to find out where He is. The four friends got in one accord to find Jesus. They operated in unity, in harmony, with one purpose and one intent: to get their friend to the healing place.

Notice that Jesus didn't say a word when there was a sudden commotion on the roof and straw or clay (or whatever the material was) started falling on the people's heads. Everyone else was wondering what was going on, thinking that those people on the roof were crazy.

There were a lot of religious people there, scribes and Pharisees. There are a lot of them around today, and they still don't like it when the roof gets taken off and the wounded and sick are brought in to Jesus. Taking off the roof makes a mess. Healing someone causes a commotion.

Religious people don't want Jesus to move in ministry because He turns things upside down. He comes against man-made religion.

Jesus apparently sat there without getting excited or saying a word. I believe He knew exactly what was going on. He knew there were men on the roof joined in unity of purpose to get to Him. He knew this incident would be read about for centuries to come and would teach something to His Church in every generation, if they would only have "an ear to hear" (Matthew 13:9).

I'm warning you: man-made traditions will keep you out of God's presence! Tradition says, "We've done it this way for a hundred years, and we are not changing now. I don't care how sick that man is, we cannot bring him down through the roof. I don't care if he ever gets healed—we cannot upset our orderly service."

We must want the Kingdom enough to "take it by force" (Matthew 11:12), the way those four men did for their friend. They took him all the way to where the glory was—even when it called for extraordinary measures! They persevered until they found a way.

Those four men exhibited another attitude we need today: they were determined to press toward the mark for the prize (Philippians 3:14). They were determined to achieve their goal.

Since our becoming one will usher in the triumphant return of Jesus Christ, achieving this "mark" or goal of reconciling the Church is the most powerful thing that can happen in this generation! Is it any wonder the devil fights to keep us from reaching the prize any way he can?

The enemy stirs up religious people to call us political, radical, extremists. He foments division, and instigates building of walls between races, classes and denominations.

The devil wants to keep us separated at all costs! One man could not have lowered the victim of palsy through the roof alone. It took four determined men working together to touch the miraculous!

The devil knows that when the Church gets together the glory of God is coming back. He is scared to death. He does not care if Catholics penetrate China, as long as they stay "on their side." He does not care if Baptists send missionaries to every continent on the globe, as long as they stay isolated from other branches of the Church. The devil fears the day we come to know that we are one in Christ. When we do, the greatest revival in the history of man will break forth—and no force on earth or below will stop it! The world will see a miracle and believe Jesus is God when they see us unified in Him.

The enemy is weakening. God is getting in some solid body blows through His Church here on earth. We are tenderizing the devil in places. Every time we come together across previous lines of division, we give the enemy a knock out blow. The Church is still in the ring and coming out for every round. Sometimes we stagger back to our "corner." However, we are never down and out for the count.

This message of reconciliation is one of the hardest to preach. People like messages about fighting against the devil or lambasting another organization. Messages "against something" are usually fiery and exciting.

But they do not like to hear messages of correction that call for changes in attitudes and works. People do not like change.

A New Cart Will Not Work

From the days of ancient Israel to the Church of today, people have blindly believed that man-made traditions (ways they are accustomed to) are "God's ways" simply because of their longevity. Anyone who comes along trying to "pull the roof off" man's traditions so the sick can get help is considered to be "coming against God!"

David's life contains a good example of the difference between the true, foundational principles of God and man-made tradition. David had a heart toward God, and he sincerely wanted his actions to be ordained, sanctioned and blessed by God. But one time he did something for God in man's way.

The ark of the covenant had been captured by the Philistines seventy years before, and David wanted to restore it to Israel. However, he did not ask God how to go about it. (Many times, the Lord will not tell you something unless you ask.) David did not check to find out how God wanted the ark to be carried. He just built a new cart and put the ark on it. As the ark proceeded down the road, it began to wobble and looked as if it might fall. When Uzzah reached out and touched the ark to steady it, he dropped dead instantly (2 Samuel 6:6). (God had warned the Israelites not to touch the ark or any holy thing in Numbers 4:15.)

Immediately, everyone became frightened, and David had sense enough to stop right there. He knew if they kept going someone else was going to die, and they would never get the ark to Jerusalem. So they left it at the house of Obed-edom the Gittite (2 Samuel 6:10). God began to bless that house, and David's heart was stirred once again to have the presence of God where it belonged. This time, however, David went to the ancient writings of Moses to find out how the ark was to be handled.

God wants the glory back in the Church. He wants a powerful Church that can move cities, towns and countries. But we have to do it His way, on His terms. He must be our Manager.

We can try all sorts of new things but that will not bring the glory back.

Different ministries and denominations have also wanted to bring back the ark (symbolic of the Lord's manifest presence), and thought they could do it. They have all learned that when man puts his hands out to touch God's glory, his own efforts all fail.

God has given us the prerequisite for revival: love one another so the world will know we are real. Instead, we send Lutheran missionaries to make Lutherans, Baptists to make Baptists, Pentecostals to make Pentecostals. We have "built new carts" to carry the glory, but it will not work.

I'm sure David asked the priests, "Why did God smite Uzzah but bless Obed-edom? What happened? Where did we do wrong?" They read the scrolls of Moses and found that the ark was not supposed to be on a cart at all. Sanctified priests were to carry the ark on wooden staves covered with gold. Wood symbolizes flesh, but gold symbolizes divinity. God wants to take flesh, overlay it with Himself, and make it divine. He wants to cover the Church with His glory. David and the priests found out what they had been doing wrong. They went line by line through the Word of God to find out what must be done to carry the ark God's way.

We must study "the whole Book" to find out what must be done to bring healing to the Church and the nations. We need to stop making up our own ways, and calling them God's.

I believe the men who went back to Obed-edom's house to get the ark were desperately praying, "Oh, Lord, we have done all of this at Your Word and for Your glory. Don't smite us, Lord. If we have done anything wrong—anything that is not pleasing—say it now, Lord."

We should feel the same way. We must back up and look at our mistakes, then find out exactly how God wants things done. If we continue to hold on to our empty man-made traditions, and insist upon the old traditional ways, the sheep will continue to "drop dead" by the wayside because we are trying to carry what is holy in unholy vessels. God meant for ministers of all churches and denominations to carry the "ark" on their shoulders. We will have to operate in the same kind of unity demonstrated by the four friends who brought the palsied man to Jesus. We can only move forward as each of us agrees to walk in the same direction.

When David and his men went to get the ark, they were all in one accord and in proper order according to the law. Then the glory of God fell upon them and they all began to rejoice.

With every step, they laughed, and sang and danced with joy. King David got so caught up in the glory that he took off his crown and kingly robes and danced in the road with the rest of them. They all rejoiced because the glory was coming back (2 Samuel 6:14-15).

Would you like to see this in our time? I long to see enough of God's people get together to "carry" His Kingdom, His Church, where it should be. Not one man—not one ministry or one denomination—but all the Church of Jesus Christ putting their shoulders to the ark, carrying their weight, fulfilling their responsibilities.

When this happens, we will see the joy and glory of the Lord as we have never seen them before. There will be a holy joy, a holy laughter, a holy dance. Yes, there will be those like David's wife, Michal, who will look at us from a distance in scorn (2 Samuel 6:16, 20-23). They will say, "Look at them! Dancing in the streets, making fools of themselves." There will always be those who scorn the joy of others. But I say, dance on, brethren! Dance on!

The Holy Spirit is at work among us. Godly leaders from all organizations, groups and systems are pressing toward the unity required to return the ark where it belongs. God has assigned me to "search the Book" and not lose sight of the goal until His glory has been restored to the Church.

His Glory Can Be Seen

Isaiah 40:5 says that God's glory can be seen: *"And the glory of the Lord shall be revealed, and all flesh shall see it together: for the mouth of the Lord hath spoken it."*

God's glory is not merely an abstract or intangible concept. It is real and can be seen. Exodus 24:7 says His glory is a devouring fire. Exodus 40:34 says it is like a cloud that filled the tabernacle. It filled the temple Solomon built (1 Kings 8:10). Since Jesus came, God's children have literally become the Temple of God (1 Corinthians 3:16). Our homes should be filled with the glory of God because we are there!

Psalm 19:1 says the heavens declare His glory. In that verse, the Hebrew word translated *declare* means "proclamation," a statement that is announced to the public. The heavens make a statement to the world of God's glory, declaring all that He is.

Luke 2:9 says His glory shines forth. Later, in Acts 7:55, Luke described Stephen as he saw "the glory of God" in his martyrdom. What did Stephen see? He saw Jesus standing at the right hand of God.

When we catch a real glimpse of the glory of God, we will have a revelation of Jesus, the Son of God, burning in our hearts. Paul says in 2 Corinthians 3:18 that we see the glory as in a glass or mirror. That verse can be translated: "Christians changed into His image day by day have no veils of darkness over their faces. Like mirrors, they reflect the glory of the Lord."

People should be able to see the glory of God in our faces. We are supposed to be the reflection of His glory. I know some people who spend so much time with the Lord that His glory is on their faces. I can feel the power of God by being with them. God's glory cannot be hidden, it will show forth. We are to be open epistles (letters to the people) ready to be studied. Without unity, the Church will not be able to win the world.

If you have heard the call to unity and believe this message, then I must tell you there is a price to pay. We cannot "play church" any longer. You will be tried in the fire. The middle rounds of this fight may prove to be the toughest.

THE MIDDLE ROUNDS:
Spiritual Warfare

For though we walk in the flesh, we do not war after the flesh:

(For the weapons of our warfare are not carnal, but mighty through God....)

1 Corinthians 10:3-4

Thou therefore endure hardness, as a good soldier of Jesus Christ.

No man that warreth entangleth himself with the affairs of this life; that he may please him who hath chosen him to be a soldier.

2 Timothy 2:3-4

There Is a Price to Pay

In the nineties, men and women of God must pay the price; we must decide if we are serious about church or only "playing." The Church is going to come under a strong attack because of those who preach the Word of God without compromise. When strong preaching comes against traditions or the established ways of society, persecution always comes.

Jewish stories say that Isaiah preached so strongly against the idolatrous, ungodly ways of the cultural, civil and religious establishments in his day that King Manasseh had him tied between two planks and sawed in half (Hebrews 11:37).

Isaiah was a statesman as well as a prophet. He was reportedly of the royal family of David, as was Daniel. He was a man of authority who dealt with spiritual and governmental issues through the reigns of five different kings. He was held in great respect, but was martyred by Manasseh in the end because he refused to compromise.

The whole Church is going to come under great scrutiny in the times to come. If a law is passed with the goal of restricting any religion, even the cults, to be "democratic" it will have to affect all religions, all churches. Christians today are walking to the right and to the left, and some are walking gingerly down the middle. Laws will be passed to discriminate against all of us.

In these times, we only have two choices: stand up and be counted for Jesus, accepting the persecution; or renounce the Lord and be counted with the world. Jesus said if you are not for Him, you are against Him (Matthew 12:30). There is no middle or neutral ground.

The devil hates the Church, the Body of Jesus Christ. His desire has always been to have mankind worship him, even as he tried to get Jesus to bow before him. He will do anything and everything to destroy the Church of the Lord Jesus Christ.

I want to say to brethren in denominations or churches that have nothing to do with each other that we had better get together soon. It will be too late if we are ever put up against a wall before a firing squad. It will be too late to ask, "Why didn't we get together before now?"

We may not have a country to have discussions in if we do not hurry up and get this nation turned back to God. This nation was founded and destined by God to follow a certain track, but it has been derailed by the humanistic element. The humanists propagate "the big lie," with labels and slogans that sound so pleasing and right, yet mean something totally different. For example, who could object or find offense in "the Day of the Child?" We had better get the literature on this move and find out what that really means!

On every continent, individuals and groups whose highest god is man, are trying to turn children into monsters, placing responsibilities on children that belong to parents. Although the communist system has already proven that it has not worked over the past seventy years, determined groups driven by this philosophy continue their efforts to destroy the home by turning the authority over children to the state.

On the other hand, we should not fear. We need to remember that God is our "shield and buckler," our strength. A person really is never alone, if he is born again. The Holy Spirit is ever present to provide comfort and strength. There is a spirit of fear abroad in the land today. This is part of the increased attacks on humanity by the enemy.

Isaiah 12:3 says, "with joy shall you draw waters." He was talking about drawing from the Living Water, the Holy Spirit. The law of gravity makes it harder to pull something up than let it down. It is easier to "let down the bucket" by crying, "Lord, help me." But we need to press in and pray in the Spirit to raise the bucket until the water overflows.

We must preserve the free nations. I live in America, which has been a beachhead for Christianity like no other nation in the history of the world. Even Israel in ancient times did not uphold God to the rest of the world the way the United States and Great Britain have. We have more preachers, have sent more missionaries and have given more money than any other nation. We have produced the Gospel in every possible way: printed media, radio, and television, as well as preaching and teaching. The free nations of the world are God's pulpits. The Church had better clean up its act before the devil shuts us down. Judgment begins at the house of the Lord (1 Peter 4:17). For two hundred years, Americans have been declaring that they are God's people with liberty and justice for all. We Americans have enjoyed freedom of religion as few nations have. Now, God is saying to America, "Don't preach one thing and live another. Don't say 'in God we trust,' if that is a lie."

If America does not put a stop to abortion and change all other demonically inspired laws that are being passed against God, He will send His wrath on this nation.

God Will Meet Our Needs

America is already losing the blessings of God, just as other nations have lost God's blessings when they turned their hearts away. A spirit of divisiveness has come to destroy national unity. People are fighting for their culture or ancestry instead of wanting to be healed as a united people. The blessings of God are fading. Our economy is failing, violence is increasing, there are "wild beasts" in the streets, and ungodly life styles are resulting in the most murderous plague (AIDS) ever known to mankind.

The United States was blessed until after World War I because its founding fathers realized that God was all-sufficient and their greatest need was to know and follow Him. As long as we do that, He will supply all of our needs according to His riches in glory (Philippians 4:19). If we seek Him and not things, God will meet our needs. God blessed America because its men were not ashamed to call on the name of the Lord. They were not ashamed to proclaim themselves a nation under God. They made statements for God by putting His name on their money and public buildings. It was not in their resources or their money that they trusted in earlier days; their trust was in God. When we lose that trust, we begin to run short. If we put our trust in God, He will meet our needs. Any country which returns to what the Word of God says can get out of debt.

The unity in America from the beginning was based on God's Word. That one thing—freedom to worship God, each in His own way—was the desire of all who came to America in the early days. When America began to lose her unity of purpose, based on the call of God, she began to lose her blessings.

The Great Depression in the thirties was a huge warning to the Church to begin to pray and turn America from its ungodly ways. Instead of intercession, the Church did two things: it agreed with humanism, and began to talk about God's coming to rapture her out of this sinful world. The American church gave our country to the enemy. We abdicated our place in civil affairs and our responsibility to carry out the mandate in Genesis 1:28 to "be fruitful, and multiply, and replenish the earth, and subdue it: and have dominion over the fish of the sea, and over the fowl of the air, and over every living thing that moveth upon the earth." We blindly joined with those who wanted to separate church and state in order to get rid of the Church. We played right into their hands.

Things have progressed to such an extent, there is a real price to pay for those who stand up and try to turn this nation around. We must be like Isaiah, willing to be martyred in order not to compromise the Word of God. During this century, the Church in the Western hemisphere has progressively watered down her message, falling into the cultures and patterns of the world.

We who are totally committed to the will of God need to understand spiritual warfare more than ever. We need to be genuine spiritual soldiers, moving from a "holding action" that has led to our gradual loss of ground and actively attack to regain territory. For that reason, God is raising up His soldiers, His army. The battle is real!

God Trains Soldiers

God is the one who trains soldiers, the one who chooses men. No one can come to the Father unless the Holy Spirit draws him. God's choosing is not according to man's thinking or desires. He knows the heart, the kind of material He needs in order to develop faithful men and women.

God's selection is not like man's. In 1 Corinthians 1:26-29, God chooses the weak things of the world to confound those that are mighty. If we chose according to the flesh, we would turn that around. Usually, men do choose "the mighty" to lead.

For ye see your calling, brethren, how that not many wise men after the flesh, not many mighty, not many noble are called:

But God hath chosen the foolish things of the world to confound the wise; and God hath chosen the weak things of the world to confound the things which are mighty;

And base things of the world, and things which are despised, hath God chosen, yea, and things which are not, to bring to naught things that are:

That no flesh should glory in His presence.

Anyone who thinks he is going to get into the ministry or become an "officer" in the Kingdom of God without going through the furnace of affliction had better re-evaluate his thinking. Without being chosen, trained and tested in the fire of God, your ministry is but a career, and you are but a hireling (John 10:12-13). Hirelings run when the wolf comes, because their hearts are not to protect the sheep.

There is a price to pay to become a warrior, a fighter for God. We have to learn God's "boxing techniques" and principles. Christ will lead you into the furnace. There are a lot of teachings and praise songs in the Church today about everything being lovely and victorious if you have enough faith. However, if we follow God in a committed, dedicated, sold-out way, we will be singing those songs in the fiery furnace! God never stops training, refining and firming up His soldiers. We will come out like pure gold if we stick with the "training program."

When we were doing the Miami for Jesus Rally in 1981, Arthur Blessit was leading the march with the big cross he has carried around the world. Former Los Angeles Ram, Rosey Grier, and others were taking turns carrying it down the street. I said, "Let me carry that a little while," but I did not know what I was asking! That thing dug into my shoulder, but I did not want anyone to know I was hurting. I bit my lip and my tongue and could not hold a conversation. It was all I could do to get enough breath to take the next step.

When you are carrying a cross, your walk is a lot harder. Some people want to make it through the Christian walk without carrying a cross and refuse to pass through the furnace.

When God speaks, we must get up and go where He says, or we will sit down and go nowhere. If we begin to argue and question, God will pass us by and move to the next person.

Obedience without questioning is one area that God teaches His soldiers. Abraham is the classic example. God told Abraham to leave his home town and family and he did so without question (Genesis 12:1). He did not say, "Why? Can't I do your will here just as well? Where do You want me to go? How am I going to get there? Where is the transportation? Are you going to provide the finances?" All God told Abraham was to leave where he was and go to a land that God would show him. Sometimes God will tell His soldiers to do something without giving the whole picture. He only gives us information on a step-by-step, "need-to-know" basis.

Some Christians in this computer age want everything mapped out ahead of time "in triplicate." We want angels, signs and confirmations. Sometimes God gives us an assignment, then waits to see what we are going to do about it. When we begin to move, He may say, "Just keep walking. I'll tell you the rest when I want you to know." We must keep moving until we hear from Him again.

Some ministries want to "build castles." Don't build some big castle that you cannot leave. Buy yourself a tent that you can fold up whenever He says to move. Otherwise, you may miss God and be left behind.

God sent Moses to bring His people out of Egypt, but Moses is not a good example of how to follow God's directions in complete obedience, at least not in the beginning. He was afraid and kept making excuses until God became angry with him and sent his brother Aaron to help (Exodus 4:14). Later, after Moses saw God's deliverance, he became a changed man, one of the mightiest men God ever had. It is much better to obey as Abraham did.

God wants every soldier to be a willing and obedient servant. God has people living in bondage everywhere, even in the most backward tribes and nations. If those whom He calls will step out and go, souls will be saved. Many are in hell because someone did not obey God when He told them to leave their home and family and go to a land that He would show them.

If you have houses, lands, jobs, education, positions, or anything that would keep you from being obedient and moving into the will of God, get rid of it! It is more important to follow Jesus.

Stay Busy in the Lord's Work

When God looks for someone to do a special assignment, He looks for someone who is busy, faithful and obedient. When God looked for someone to replace Elijah, He found a man plowing, being faithful with his parents' fields, someone who was already busy doing something. God does not pick lazy people. Elisha was plowing at his assigned job, minding his own business. There were people all around that could have been chosen. Many prophets were in schools, following Elijah around, but God did not pick one of them. When Elijah threw his mantle down, he placed his authority over Elisha (1 Kings 19:19). Elisha accepted the authority of Elijah over him.

If a man refuses and rejects authority, he also in essence rejects the anointing. God does not anoint rebellion. We must be under authority. If a man will not submit to authority, he has no right to demand submission from anyone else. Many times young preachers get an attitude that they do not need anyone to tell them anything. The first thing you know, they are on the phone yelling, "Help!" All of us need to be under authority, or we are nothing but rebels. The Word of God says "rebellion is as the sin of witchcraft" (1 Samuel 15:23), and God will not anoint witchcraft.

Elisha immediately dropped the lines on the oxen and said, "Wait a minute! Let me just go and tell my parents goodbye." Elijah said, "Go ahead, do what you want. It is your choice." Suppose Elisha's parents had begun to pull on him, not wanting him to go. He may have been the only son, at least the oldest. But he was not going to let anything hold him back from the call of God.

The Bible says that he chopped up the plows and killed the oxen, making a farewell feast for the workers on the farm. He was "burning his bridges behind him" (1 Kings 19:21). Elisha said, "No turning back for me. I have felt the mantle of the prophet upon me, the call of God. I know what I must do, and mother, father, work, goals, or whatever I had planned for the future is gone."

The Apostle Paul did the same thing. He was a man of letters, had a keen intellect, a reputation with the leaders of his nation, respect and position. But when he met Jesus, he left everything else behind.

Some Christians are like Ananias and Sapphira (Acts 5:1-11), holding a little something back "in case God fails." God is our employer, as well as our Manager, and He will never fail. He knows our needs. There are many in the ministry who are investing in the things of the world today instead of totally trusting God.

When we first moved to Virginia Beach, a well-known young preacher called to make an appointment with me. He said, "I want to introduce you to something that is going to secure your future. This is a new thing where you buy in and become a stockholder. Then you get other people to do the same thing, making money on those people. In the ministry, people do not want to pay you right, or take care of you. People begrudge you anything you make," he said, going on and on. He sounded so good that it seemed I would be foolish not to invest. Being young, I tried the investment and that venture

cleaned me out. It took everything I had and naturally I complained to God. He said, "I didn't call you to be a Wall Street
manipulator or to go into business. I didn't call you to do anything that will distract you from my anointing and my call on
your life. I called you to preach the gospel of Jesus Christ, and
you will have no other employment."

Jesus is not only our Savior, Healer and Deliverer, He is our
Provider also!

Everything depends on who you trust: Wall Street, the wel-
fare system, your employer, the Social Security system, or the
God who has never failed. Who do *you* trust the most?

One way God trains His soldiers is to see if they will serve
Him when their needs are not being plentifully met. Paul said
that he had been "abased" (that means poor and humbled) and
he had "abounded," which means he had plenty (Phillippians
4:12). He did not always have a lot, but he always made it. God
never forsakes us.

When Anne and I first began in the ministry, we did not have
nice cars, good clothes, or even our own place to live. People
left bags of food at our door for us to find when we came home.
It has not been all "gravy." Sometimes we were not certain that
we would get our salary of $25 a week, but we stuck with God.
In good times and bad times, we have never given up, but we
have always found a way to give out of what we had.

I truly believe some preachers today are not submitting to
God's training. They expect to be waited on hand and foot and
treated like royalty. Pastors are to be servants of the people. If
they serve, God will bless them. His soldiers must understand
that they serve the people.

Stabbed With Your Own Sword

Soldiers for Jesus also need to learn that the devil likes to
stab them with their own "sword." The best way to destroy a
man's message is to get him to fail in that area. Your strongest

point can also be your weakest. For example, if a man is called to preach righteousness, the enemy will try to get him to be unrighteous. Then all those years of labor and ministering are lost. Many of the people who heard the message may fall away and say, "If that message is true, why didn't he abide by it?"

One minister came to Rock Church and preached about marriage relationships. A few years later, he left his wife and the church he was pastoring. He backslid and left the ministry. Today, his wife who stood firm and faithful in the gospel is now the pastor of the church her husband left. She is doing a great job! The enemy is always trying to get a man to fail in the very area of emphasis that God has given him.

God has given my ministry the message of unity, so the enemy would love to get us entangled in a fight or feud. For example, a few months ago, a certain man said some terrible things about us and other leaders in the Charismatic movement on a television program.

When we heard it, we thought about suing him. We talked to our lawyer, and prepared to file an injunction to stop the man from continuing with the lies.

Later, Anne and I were in a meeting with the attorney when the Spirit of the Lord suddenly spoke to me and said, "Be careful with the fly." Those five little words taught me a volume! So I said, "Brother, I want you to write a letter to that man and tell him we are aware of what he is doing, and to consider the fact that what he is saying is not true. Tell him we are praying for him, that we love him, and we believe God will strengthen and bless him. And that is it. Let it go at that."

The Holy Spirit's reference to the fly concerned a time when a fly began to buzz around me as I was preaching. I was building up to my main point and getting ready to really put it across. Everyone was waiting to hear where I was going with the message. There was a great anointing. Then that fly appeared! The fly kept buzzing around and I lost my whole message as well as the anointing by trying to swat it. A wise brother told me, "Brother John, if you leave flies alone, they will go away. But if you pay attention to them, they will hang around a lot longer."

There are a whole lot of bees, flies, hornets and such flying around in the Church world today. Ignore them! God does not train His soldiers to sit around on the sidelines swatting flies. He trains them to move into warfare. We need to learn how to battle, but sometimes the wisest thing to do is to ignore the fly and pay attention to the lion that's roaring. We have much to learn about this fight.

Round 6

God's Army
Must Learn How to Battle

Every soldier must learn the tactics and techniques of warfare, but the desire to fight and the determination to win must come from the heart and soul. First, you must know that a thing has to be done, and then you set your will to do the best you can. Then you learn how to fight.

Think what would happen to someone like you or me if we stepped into the ring with a champion like Muhammed Ali? What if that person did not want to fight and didn't even know he was in a fight? That is where many Christians are today. They either do not know there is a battle, or they think if they remain quiet, ignore the devil, and avoid stirring him up, he will ignore them. That is foolishness.

On the other hand, even someone with the greatest heart to fight and the willingness to "come out slugging," would still lose without training. If he tried to take on Ali, he might be knocked out in the first round. If he did not know boxing techniques, he would not last long in the ring. In spite of a great heart to fight, he would get whipped.

God not only chooses soldiers, but He trains them for the battle—if they submit to His management. No one can be trained in anything against his will. A soldier must learn to use what God has given him, and the local church is God's "training camp." Remember, God established the Church to demonstrate His wisdom to the enemy (Ephesians 3:10-11). Jesus defeated satan, yet his evil works still linger, foster and multiply in our lives. They must be destroyed. There is no peace treaty, no neutrality. I preached once about the SALT (Strategic Arms Limitation Treaties) Treaties, and said they are not going to work. The only SALT Treaty that will work is the original one: **Ye are the salt of the earth** (Matthew 5:13).

A soldier going into war is going to get hurt, if not killed, if he does not prepare himself for the battle. He must listen to instructions, then he must practice. If someone backslides, it happens because he was not listening or not practicing what he was taught.

One of the first things a boxing trainer tells his student is to keep his hands up at all times. Stay ready to punch your opponent. Don't be naive. Once you enlist in God's army by choosing to be born again, you are in the ring. When you "put on God's colors," you become a target. You will only get out of the ring in a coffin or as a champion. If you do not have your hands up ready to deflect the blows of the enemy and counter punch, he will knock you out.

A boxer practices the techniques he has learned. He gets in the ring and jabs, bobs and weaves. Why does he do that? So that he will avoid his opponent's blows and not get knocked out. He practices throwing punches at a bag until he perfects his punch.

The Holy Spirit is the recruiting officer. He woos you, then He speaks to your heart. God has given us the Bible which contains all the rules of the "ring" of life. If you do not study it and practice it, you will get knocked out. You are not in the world to hobnob with the world. You are here as a soldier. You are here to conquer and expand the territory the Kingdom occupies.

King Jesus already owns the earth, but we are to possess territory for Him.

In addition to studying the rules and practicing your punches, you must be obedient to the Commander-in-Chief (Joshua 5:13-15). James 1:22 tells us that we must be doers of the Word and not just hearers. Being obedient means doing what you are told to do. If we don't do what the Word says, we are disobedient to God. On the other hand, misplaced zeal can play into your opponent's hands. He can use your unbalanced momentum to defeat you.

I remember a woman who went about "warfare" the wrong way. This lady was saved in my church. Her husband was a good-looking man who worked in a bank and liked a couple of beers at night. She became so zealous to get him saved that she decided to go to the refrigerator and pour out all his beer. He came home and wanted to know where his beer was, and she told him she was not having beer in the house. Of course, he was angry. She came to me then, asking if she had done the right thing. I said, "If it had been me in my old days, I might have popped you in the eyeball. You go right now and buy a six-pack and give it back to him. He bought the beer, not you. He's your husband, not your child."

I pointed out to her that she was not going to save her husband—it would have to be the Holy Spirit. How could the Spirit reach her husband's heart when she was usurping his authority? He had been drinking beer when they met and married. He had not changed—she had! She could not force him to conform to her. He had to want to conform to Jesus. I was not defending the beer, but her attitude and actions were turning her husband against her, the church, and God. That attitude could have resulted in divorce and possibly hell for him. By imposing her will, she could cause him to never want to follow Jesus. She was fighting flesh with flesh, instead of going to her knees and fighting flesh with spirit (1 Peter 3:1).

Know Your Enemies

That same lady, several years later, called to give me "a word from God." She had left her husband because he was "not spiritual enough." She had taken the children and gone to Florida. We had counseled her against that because her husband was a good man who loved and provided for her. We told her to pray and wait for God to save him. However, she said, "I don't love him. I love Jesus, and I don't need him." She was going to do whatever she wanted, regardless of what anyone said.

This kind of boxer always loses, because he or she won't take the counsel of the manager. He thinks he can win the battle on his own.

This particular lady now floats around from state to state and place to place. One day after she left Virginia, I received a call from the pastor of a church in Florida asking about her. I told him she had attended my church but had moved. He said, "She's here now, and she has gathered a little group around her that meets and prophesies over one another. She has prophesied that my wife was going to die, and then she would be my wife."

People with rebellious spirits are spiritual lepers. Their contamination spreads to others. God did not appoint them to be pastors or leaders, but they think they know more than God.

I told the pastor who called that she had been in my church, but that she would not submit to us or to her husband. I advised him not to pay any attention to her. She had no stability and would not submit to spiritual authority. He apparently told her what I said because she called me and was angry. I said, "I'm sorry you're upset, but I just told the man the truth."

Some years later she called and said God had given her a "word" for Anne and me. She said, "Brother John, you know I love you and Sister Anne, but God gave me a word for you. God told me to give you Jeremiah 23:1: Woe be unto pastors that destroy and scatter the sheep of my pasture! saith the Lord."

I was not about to take her "word" seriously, because I knew her life style and her heart. I told her that God had not given me that scripture. She said she had been in our area recently and had visited several people from the church. She named several discontented people from the church. She had visited troublemakers, those who would not come into unity with the rest of the church. (They were out of fellowship and in a state of rebellion spreading the disease of leprosy).

This woman did not visit the church itself to see the glory, the moving of God, and the joy of the Lord in our services. She spent her time visiting rebels. She had no word from the Lord. If God cannot get through to me directly about something I am doing, He is going to send a real prophet to speak to me. He is not going to send someone who has left her husband and runs around the country prophesying false prophecies. The Bible says you will know what spirit a person is by his fruit (Matthew 7:16). That lady is no longer fighting the enemy. She has gone over to his corner to help him out!

We are in a war that is greater than the one Alexander the Great fought. It is greater than World Wars I and II. We are talking about a battle that will affect mankind for all eternity. This one began before Creation and will end when the enemy is confined forever to the lake of fire (Revelation 20:10). We must know our enemy and our targets. Warfare involves both defense and offense.

Our first target is the flesh. Holiness is our weapon against the flesh, and it comes from the inside, not the outside. Not everything that tempts a person or causes problems comes from the devil. A lot of it comes from our flesh. Galatians 5:17 shows us there is constant combat between the spirit and the flesh. Your spirit is in one corner with God the ultimate Champion as trainer, and your flesh is in the other corner with the devil as trainer. If your spirit-man has been trained to resist the devil and conduct effective spiritual warfare, there is no contest. Your spirit, in union with God's spirit, will win, because your Trainer is greater than the one in the world (1 John 4:4).

After an Indian chief became born again, he would praise the Lord, be happy and loving, and hug everyone one day, and the next, he would be grouchy, grumpy and downcast. Everyone wondered what was wrong. Finally one of the braves asked him, "Chief, what is wrong with you? Sometimes you are the nicest guy in the world, then sometimes you walk around looking like you want to kill someone." The chief said, "Heap big fight going on—two dogs fight inside me. One is a pretty little white dog, and the other is a bad, red dog that snarls all the time. When white dog comes, he is gentle and makes me gentle. When red dog comes, he make me mad and angry." The other brave asked, "Chief, which dog is gonna win the fight?" The chief said, "The one I feed the most will win the fight."

If we feed ourselves with things of the flesh, then the flesh will win that round. If we fill ourselves with the things of God and His righteousness, the spirit man will be the winner.

Our second target is the devil. Ephesians 6:12 says that we do not "wrestle" against flesh and blood, but against the demon spirits within people. The Bible says much about the devil, primarily how to deal with him. Resist him, rebuke him and cast him out. Those are the three methods Jesus used to combat the enemy.

The Bible says he is as a roaring lion seeking something to devour. Notice that it does not say the devil is a roaring lion, because Jesus pulled his teeth. However, the devil roars loud enough sometimes to make a man shake in his boots.

A lot of Christians walk around as if there were no lion roaring in the background. What would it be like to walk down a street late at night and suddenly hear a lion roar nearby? As Christians, we ought to be aware that this is how we walk all of the time. There is always a lion roaring.

We do not have to fear. We can wrestle him to the ground through prayer or stab him with the sword of the Spirit because Jesus pulled satan's teeth. We can rebuke him and send him running with his tail between his legs. We cannot ignore him, because he can still defeat us.

The Word of God says:

Be sober, be vigilant; because your adversary the devil, as a roaring lion, walketh about, seeking whom he may devour:

Whom resist stedfast in the faith, knowing that the same afflictions are accomplished in your brethren that are in the world. (Your brothers in Christ are experiencing the same kinds of attacks.)

1 Peter 5:8-9

Our third target is "the world," which means the systems that were inspired and formed by the devil. James 4:4 says:

Know ye not that the friendship of the world is enmity with God.

Enmity means to "cut oneself off" from someone. That is the opposite of what any Christian wants to do with God. Friendship with the world means friendship with the devil. That puts us "at enmity" with God, it makes us His enemy. We can go to church during the week, but if we "hang out" with the world, affiliate with the world, and act like the world, we will become an enemy of God.

We should be in the place with God that anytime we see the world's systems in operation, our nostrils flare, our muscles tense up, and we are ready to go into combat. That is why I go into a combat-ready stance whenever abortion is mentioned, for it is contrary to the laws of God.

Our enemies in the world are not the people, but the spirits behind them and in them. We must hate what is of the world.

We cannot go into war saying, "I do not want to hurt anyone." We must set out to hurt satan and all his troops. We cannot go into spiritual warfare with any thoughts of peace treaties, negotiation or "co-existence." It must be all or nothing. We know that the Church has won, but in our individual battles we can still win or lose.

Someone said to me one day, "You do not have to preach so hard against the world." I said, "What are you talking about? I'm not preaching against the world, God is. I am repeating what He said in His Word. We agree with the world when we watch movies formulated in hell: monsters, violence, demonic entities or cannibalistic films, to mention just a few. Dracula is very popular today. In fact, there is a spirit of Dracula loose in the land, and vampirism is a counterfeit of the blood covenant. There are musical groups dressing and acting like Dracula. There even are comedies made out of this myth! To take a satanic theme and make it seem harmless and funny is more horrible than the horror films.

The enemy inspires people to do these things to disarm God's people, so they will say, "Oh, well, it's popular. They are just movies, or just toys or just games. Everyone else is doing it, so it must be all right. All the children have these toys, so my child will feel different and deprived if I keep them from him."

They are not harmless! It is better to have your child feeling "deprived" than to have him demonized and perhaps, later, refuse Jesus and go to hell because of these influences.

The battle is not only in the church building, but it is in the church home, it is in the family structure and in our society. If the Church is going to live in victory, it must become knowledgeable of these demonic influences and overcome them.

Round 7

Ten Steps
of Spiritual Warfare

The life and ministry of Jesus contain the greatest episode and example of spiritual warfare in all creation; but He provides most of our information concerning spiritual warfare through Paul's epistles to the churches. The Apostle Paul shows us that there is still a fight, who our enemy is, and how to defeat him. One of the most significant passages on spiritual warfare is in 2 Corinthians 10:3-5:

For though we walk in the flesh, we do not war after the flesh:

(For the weapons of our warfare are not carnal, but mighty through God to the pulling down of strong holds;)

Casting down imaginations, and every high thing that exalteth itself against the knowledge of God, and bringing into captivity every thought to the obedience of Christ;

Anything in our lives that tries to exalt itself above God needs to be pulled down. If we do not pull it down, it will knock us down. Anything that interferes with us reading the scriptures, praying, and seeking the will of God has got to be eliminated.

If you follow these instructions of warfare, you can do what Paul says in Ephesians 6:11-13. We must direct our prayer against principalities, powers, rulers of the darkness of this world, and spiritual wickedness in high places, instead of against mere flesh and blood. We must discipline our own flesh and bring it into submission, so that we do not spend a lot of time dealing with ourselves.

Paul's letter to the Ephesians tells us to put on the whole armor of God in order to stand in the evil day. There are ten fundamental steps of spiritual warfare that will help you put on your armor and stand.

Vision, Goal, and Headquarters

The first step is vision.

God is a reality. Those who have "seen" God are strongest in their desire to know Him intimately. We must have a "vision" of the reality of His righteousness, His purpose, and of all that He is doing today. If we go into war not knowing our Commander and His cause, we will have no real will to win.

The second step is to have a goal.

If we do not have a goal, we are lost. We cannot run the race until we "set a mark." We must have something to shoot at. In natural warfare, you first must have a goal or point to attack. Then you start maneuvering to reach your goal and eventually to conquer.

My friend and I were invited as guests for a Navy orientation cruise. We loaded our suitcases full of tracts. Everyone else headed for the cocktail lounge once they were aboard, because their goal was to have a good time. Our goal was to do something for the Lord.

While the other guests and officers were "boozing," we distributed tracts. We put them in all the bathrooms so that a person had to pick up a tract to use a commode or latrine. Someone complained about us, and the captain told the chaplain to find us and make us stop what we were doing. Meanwhile, we talked to the sailors and passed out tracts while everyone else was watching plane maneuvers. The chaplain told us what we were doing was illegal, but we did not know that.

He began to ask us questions about ourselves and our doctrines. We were the wrong pair for him to question about our beliefs! Before long, we had our hands on that man's head, and were praying and shaking him around. He soon began to speak with other tongues, and we had a revival right there! He caught a vision of God and set a new goal for himself. Soon men were getting saved on that ship.

Some years later, I was preaching in Rochester, New York, when two young men came up to me and said, "Hello, Brother Gimenez." I said, "Hello. How are you? Praise the Lord," but I did not remember ever seeing them before. They said, "You don't remember us? We were on the *U.S.S. Lexington* when you made the cruise." "You were?" I asked. They said yes, and told me what happened after my friend and I made our "orientation" trip. The chaplain began to move in the Lord.

At one point, the ship veered off course and it looked like they were going to miss a strategic rendezvous. The captain jokingly said, "Hey, Reverend! Could you pray and see if God will do something about this wind, because we are going to be late?" The chaplain took it seriously and began to pray, "God, You are the Creator of the winds. We ask You to straighten out the winds. Put them behind us, instead of giving us a head wind." That is exactly what happened! The winds changed, and they reached their destiny on time. Needless to say, that captain had a new respect for the prayers of the chaplain.

Make sure your goal is in line with God's plan for your life.

The third step is to have a headquarters, a base from which to operate.

People who do the most for God belong to a local church. They have a headquarters, a place of support.

Not long ago, we had some young people stop by our church. They said they were Christians, and had no money. "Father told us to come here. Could you help us? (They never said 'Jesus'; they said 'Father.') We don't have a place to stay, and we are hungry." There were seven of them traveling together, four men and three girls, but they were not married. As far as I am concerned, that violated Paul's admonition to "abstain from all the appearance of evil" (1 Thessalonians 5:22). I offered to arrange lodging for the girls in one place and the boys in another.

They said, "Oh, no! Father told us not to separate. We have to sleep in the same place." I said, "Well, my Father says no." Then I asked who their pastor was, and they said, "What do you mean?" I said, "Who is your shepherd, your pastor? What church do you belong to?"

They said, "We do not have a pastor. We do not belong to a church."

I asked "Who teaches you? Who protects you?" "Nobody," they answered.

Then I tried to find out where they came from, and they told me, "Here and there; everywhere." Finally I said, "I'm sorry, but you have me in a predicament." I gave them $20 and told them to go eat. I offered again to put them up in separate places, or to take in the girls, but they refused.

Without a base of support, people like this will never have victory in their lives. I want to make a statement here that I know will probably stir up some anger. But I truly believe that any so-called ministry that is not under the oversight of a local church is out of God's order and eventually will become a force against the local church. Para-church ministries are not scriptural. Jesus did not say "upon this rock I will build my para-church."

We have military bases in our area. When church members in the military are sent overseas, we have them come to the front and we pray over them. We do not just pray over missionaries or pastors sent out from the church. Many times military men and women who left our church for deployment have literally started revivals on board their ships.

We all need a base of operations, a place we can point to as home. I tell everyone to get under a good pastor. Go to church somewhere and get under some ministry. Without the five-fold ministry, we cannot be perfected (Ephesians 4:11-13). Without a home base, we will never bring forth lasting fruits of righteousness.

Morale, concentration of resources, and good stewardship:

The fourth step is to maintain morale.

We must not let ourselves come under depression, discouragement or heaviness. We must maintain our joy and not get downhearted. We can do all things through Christ who strengthens us (Philippians 4:13). It does not matter what things look like, we can win. We are more than conquerors through Christ Jesus (Romans 8:37).

Keep your spirits up. Do not go around looking like you feel like dying. Feel like living, and pretty soon you will live. Remind yourself that you are seated with Jesus in heavenly places. You are working for the Lord and building His kingdom. You belong to Him. You are His child, and a joint-heir with Jesus (Romans 8:17). So why worry about the stuff down here?

The fifth step is to concentrate your resources in one place.

Bring ye all the tithes into the storehouse, that there may be meat in Mine house, and prove Me now herewith, saith the Lord of hosts, if I will not open you the windows of heaven, and pour you out a blessing, that there shall not be room enough to receive it.

Malachi 3:10

What does that mean? The **Storehouse** principle means that we do not break up our tithe into little pieces. It means bring **all** your tithes into your base of operations.

In the natural, we do the same thing. We send our taxes to Washington, D.C. The nation's resources are concentrated in one place. Suppose some Americans said, "I think I'll send my taxes to Canada," or "I'll send my taxes to Germany?" What would happen? We may not agree with the way Washington spends our taxes; nevertheless, we must send them all to one headquarters.

Some Christians send a little bit here and a little bit there. They may put some in their local churches, or they may not. That is not scriptural. We are to bring our tithes into the storehouse where we are being fed. We are to put it into our base, our storehouse. Otherwise, we cannot fight a good battle.

I believe what the prophet Malachi said concerning non-tithers. They are cursed with a curse, because they are people who are working against God's Kingdom. If it were up to them, the churches in our nation would close down. They have an anti-church spirit. They do not trust God's Word in their finances. I have no respect for them. They are thieves and robbers in the Body of Christ, yet, they often hold high positions in local churches and sometimes are the loudest complainers and troublemakers. They're cursed with a special curse.

The sixth step is to be a good steward with what you have.

We must learn to use what we have wisely. It's an abomination to God for Christians to get in debt so that they cannot pay their bills. Look at our cities, our states and our national government. New York City, the greatest city in the world, was shamed before the world by not being able to pay its bills. Other cities and towns have found themselves in the same position. Why? They were spending more than they took in. No one can keep that up indefinitely without getting into trouble. The entire country is on the verge of real disaster. We keep postponing it with this measure or the other, but someday, "all of the chickens will come home to roost."

We can extend our credit cards to pay for this and that, but in a matter of weeks, statements come that say, "Must be paid by such-and-such a date." If we do not pay, more little pieces of paper come threatening to ruin our credit report. Finally, we get an unwelcome collection letter from a lawyer. Then we may desperately wonder what we are going to do. What we should do is cut those little cards up and throw them away, because we generally can't handle having that much credit. What we buy, even on credit, must be based on what is coming in and on what we can afford to pay. If we cannot handle finances realistically, we will soon be in deep trouble.

We must learn not to use what is not ours. What we do not have, we ought not to spend. It really amounts to out-and-out robbery. If we go into someone's store and walk out with things we cannot pay for, it is stealing.

If you are having trouble handling your money, then kill your pride and admit it. There are agencies and counselors to help. Some churches, like Rock Church, have these resources available. If people ask us for help, we teach them how to make realistic budgets and live within them.

I have gotten calls from area businessmen, who say, "Why aren't these people paying their bills? They are supposed to be Christians. Why are they doing this to me?" How can I excuse those people? The businessmen are right. Christians are given admonitions and instructions in the Bible about being good stewards, about not borrowing, and about giving account for what they have. Ignorance is no excuse.

There are people who run to the church asking for help after they have messed up their own finances and cannot pay their bills. The church helps them, but they never change. They do the same things over and over again and go from church to church hustling the people of God. I can tell you many stories of people who speak in tongues, shout and dance and lift their hands in praise to God, but have no scruples about stealing from

God's house. And almost without exception, they don't practice tithing. Tithing is not just a commandment, but a weapon against the enemy. Tithing makes a way for God to bless you. When men do not tithe, Malachi 3:10 says that they are cursed with a curse.

Economy, mobility, teamwork, and security:

The seventh step is economy.

The armies that win wars are not necessarily those with the most equipment and supplies. Winning armies simply make better use of what they have.

Americans in the Revolutionary War won with no uniforms, and little food, using their own personal weapons. General George Washington and his men nearly starved to death at Valley Forge, but they still won the war—even though the British were better equipped and supplied.

Take what you have and use it wisely. Little is much when you use it to the glory of God. The widow with two mites had enough to move the heart of God (Mark 12:42)!

The widow with a little meal and oil had enough because she used it for God's man (1 Kings 17:8-16). That was spiritual warfare, for her obedience and generosity in giving to the prophet defeated the enemy's plan to kill him through Jezebel or starvation during the famine.

The two fish and five loaves (Mark 6:38) were enough to feed a multitude. That was also spiritual warfare, as God's miraculous power defeated the enemy's doubts in those who would receive the truth about whether Jesus really was the Messiah or not.

The eighth step is mobility, or flexibility.

Warfare requires mobility. We must be able to move our troops rapidly when challenges come our way. We cannot allow

ourselves to be locked into one position. God continually
moves us to new heights and depths, new dimensions, new understanding and a greater level of maturity.

Many people come to our church and really enjoy the services, yet they are not comfortable because their former church
did things differently. Those who had no flexibility could not
remain with us. The enemy could defeat them because they
would not change from traditional ways to a fresh move of God.
There was no elasticity, no stretching, no giving up of their old
wineskins for new. Jesus said putting new wine in old skins will
only cause them to burst (Matthew 9:17). We must stay young
in the things of the Lord and be able to move with what He is
doing now, not what He did yesterday. No matter how great the
latest move of God is, **we have not arrived**. There will always
be a greater move to come until Jesus Himself returns. Every
nation will confess that He is Lord of lords and King of kings
(2 Chronicles 9:5). As the Queen of Sheba said about Solomon,
the half has not yet been told.

We must remain flexible. We must be like Abraham, ready
to fold our tents and move on, not locked into living on one particular piece of ground. No army can fight that way.

The ninth step is cooperation, or teamwork.

Without teamwork, togetherness, unity and harmony, we do
not put points on the scoreboard. The Church cannot win except
as a team. I'm convinced that God has called me to work
toward unity among the brethren because we must defeat the
enemy.

No local church, family, or couple can win battles against
the flesh, the world or the devil without unity. The Church is
plagued with rivalry, competition, jealousy, and even conten-
tion today. Christians are not hearing what the Lord is saying.

If God said, "Take your shoes off, you are on holy ground,"
some would, and some would not. Some of those who did

would make a religion out of it and begin to build the denomination of the "No Shoes Church." They would lock in on that ground and begin to be defeated. Others would take the word to take off their shoes and use their obedience to glorify themselves through self-focus, self-centeredness or exhibitionism. Those who would not take off their shoes would be giving in to pride, the fear of man, or repressed emotions, and would be defeated in battle.

In any ballgame, if the team wants to win, every team member needs to follow the "leader" and do what he or she says. You can only have one quarterback. If part of the team says, "That's too hard," or "we don't feel like doing that play today," the team will lose the game. That is why many churches today are not winning battles.

The tenth step is security.

All armies have a security force that guards against unforeseen and unexpected attacks. There are many secret agents and enemy commando units that are constantly trying to penetrate the perimeters of protection that are set up. We must guard ourselves against all of the invading forces that would try to destroy us. In spiritual warfare, our enemies are described as "the works of the flesh" (Galatians 5:19-21). God has given us the armament to combat these enemies with the fruits of the Spirit (Galatians 5:22-23) and the armor of God (Ephesians 6:11).

We must guard ourselves with the shield of faith and the covering of love. Love will give us security and cushion us against hurt. "Perfect love casts out fear" (1 John 4:18). The love of God is unconditional; He loves us whether we love Him or not.

In 1 Corinthians 13, "the love chapter," we clearly see how real love is security, because it does not get hurt, resentful or rejected. Real love does not judge.

Jesus' ministry gave us the basic principles of warfare, and Paul showed us how to deal with the fight by living for the Lord. Now let's look at the three main ways that Jesus came against satan's works in His ministry.

Round 8

Ministry From God's Armory

The essence of Jesus' ministry, and the primary descriptions of spiritual warfare waged by our Commander-in-Chief, are summed up in Matthew 4:23-24:

*And Jesus went about all Galilee, **teaching** in their synagogues, and **preaching** the gospel of the kingdom, and **healing** all manner of sickness and disease among the people.*

And His fame went throughout all Syria: and they brought unto Him all sick people that were taken with divers diseases and torments, and those which were possessed with devils, and those which were lunatic, and those which had the palsy; and He healed them.

Three words describe what Jesus did: *teaching, preaching,* and *healing.* He also cast out demons, but the New Testament often refers to casting out demons as part of healing (Acts 10:38). Jesus did not go around teaching psychology or having private counseling sessions. In most denominations or seminaries today, a pastor must learn psychology, psychiatry, personality traits, and how to counsel. But Jesus did everything by *teaching, preaching and healing.*

The Bible says people were "astonished" at the authority with which He taught (Mark 1:22). Jesus did not debate or discuss different viewpoints. He knew what He was talking about, and spoke with real authority. No guesses, speculations, or maybe's. As people heard Him speak, it became obvious that He knew He was speaking the truth.

Many people begin in the ministry with a hesitant or fearful attitude, but that will not help anyone. My "father in Christ" helped me with this a long time ago. He said, "When you walk up to the pulpit, act like you are going to say something. Don't crawl. Report for duty. Don't talk so slowly that people fall asleep before you really get into the message."

Underlying Jesus' ministry was a great compassion for people. The Gospel of Mark says He was moved with compassion toward them, because they were "like sheep without a shepherd" (Mark 6:34).

If you're called to the five-fold ministry (Ephesians 4:11), you need to remember that every true minister of God must have compassion for the people. On the other hand, God is not permissive, but balanced, correcting us because He loves us. All love and no correction creates a spoiled child, and all correction without love is abuse.

Some preachers minister like they want to hit someone. Some people encourage this, as if they want to incite some kind of violence. Christians do need to be strong in warfare against their flesh, the world and demons, but they also need to be compassionate and caring toward other people.

When Jesus said, "Love your enemies" (Matthew 5:44), He spoke about people who would come against us. He is not asking us to love the devil, his troops, or his works. We should feel sorry for people, especially those without a shepherd, because they are sheep that can be easily devoured by lions and wolves, or destroyed in the wilderness—because they refuse to live under God's protective covering in the church.

There are many sheep in the Charismatic movement who feel they do not need a pastor or teacher. These people think all believers are equal to the five-fold ministry in spiritual authority because believers are told to "do the work of the ministry," but that is not true.

The "work of the ministry" is to tell the good news of Jesus, lay hands on the sick and cast out demons. The work of the five-fold ministry is to train and equip the saints, to "perfect" them for the work of the ministry (Ephesians 4:12). God has chosen to use these called-out ministries—not lay believers—to *govern* the Church.

Sheep are to reproduce more sheep—that is the work of the sheep. The "under-shepherds," the five-fold ministries under Jesus the Chief Shepherd, are to protect, feed and help the sheep grow up to make more sheep.

Jesus taught us life-changing principles from the Old Testament. He openly displayed the character and love of God the Father through His own actions, attitudes and life style: He shook the stuffy religious world to its roots with one statement: *"...He that hath seen Me hath seen the Father"* (John 14:9). He preached the good news of the Kingdom of God with authority (Luke 4:43). Teaching and preaching does no good if we do not have a valid message. We must bring Jesus to the people so that they can see Him. Most Christians have only looked into the eyes of religion or tradition, but once we "look" into the eyes of the Messiah, our lives will be changed forever.

I used to walk around in the world with my head down, not wanting to look into anybody's eyes. I did not like daylight, and I only walked the streets at night. Everything was dark: my mind, my heart and my life. Then Jesus came, and like blind Bartimaeus, I would not give up until I "saw" Him (Mark 10:46).

I was in Mountaindale, New York, in a drug rehabilitation program. We were all sleeping when I was awakened by a loud voice saying, "I rebuke you, devil. Get out of here right now! You can't take anybody out of here. We all belong to Jesus." Everybody started jumping out of bed and falling on their knees. We felt the overpowering presence of satan in that place. As I heard our leader rebuking satan, I knew that there was a battle being waged for my soul and all the souls of the men there. We are all praying and screaming at the top of our lungs demanding satan to leave. I was never so afraid in all my life. After about an hour, we felt that satanic presence leave. I got up and went out on the porch. I looked up to Heaven and began to talk to God.

I said, "God, I don't want a 'phony bologna' religion. If this is real, then prove it to me. Come into my life and change me."

Suddenly, I was on the ground with my head rolled back, screaming at the top of my lungs. I felt God's hand digging down into my chest, ripping out my old, filthy heart, and giving me a new one. He took my polluted mind and gave me a new one. I felt the genuine operation of the Holy Spirit in my life.

After God met me, I began running down the road at two o'clock in the morning. A cloud moved over me. I thought Jesus was on that cloud, and began to call Him down. My actions were utterly insane according to the world, but I had been delivered from darkness and death! I had been healed! I had seen Jesus!

Teaching, preaching and healing were the *cause* in Jesus' ministry. The **miracles, signs and wonders, healings, and deliverances** of people were the *effect*. The same pattern works today.

The Old Testament pointed to Jesus. Jesus pointed to the disciples. The disciples pointed to all of us. A gifted teacher's message never stops with his pupils. He teaches so that others will grasp the message and continue to pass the message on to those who will follow later. Paul told Timothy to *teach and exhort* the things he had heard, to commit those things to faithful men who would be able to teach others (1 Timothy 6:2; 2 Timothy 2:2).

The Message Is the Cause

On the Day of Pentecost (Acts 1, 2), the *cause* was Jesus' message for them to tarry until the Holy Spirit came. The **cause** worked, because they obeyed, fasted and prayed *in one accord*. The *effect* was the appearance of the Holy Spirit as a mighty, rushing wind and tongues of fire.

The fulfillment of God's Word also brings a visual effect. To be in Christ is to become a new creature. We should look and act differently. We cannot be Christians and remain the same as before. There must be a change. I have seen people come down to the front and cry all over the altar, then get up and be just as mean as they were before. They thought the crying somehow accomplished salvation for them.

If a man or woman is in Christ, there **has** to be a change. The Word says that He is in you and you are in Him. There is a change in newly converted people, because Jesus is **in** them. But it takes a process of making choices and letting go of things over a period of time before we truly are **in Him**.

The factor of timing must be considered between cause and effect. The 120 tarried in Jerusalem about ten days before the Holy Spirit came. The appointed time was the Day of Pentecost, the beginning of the fulfillment of the Feast of Weeks (the time of harvest). It's important to realize that Jesus did not tell them the exact time. He simply told them to "wait for it," and they obeyed.

A message received as prophecy will have an effect if it is truly from God, but it may not be manifested at once. Not long after being saved, I was at the rehabilitation farm in Mountaindale, and someone prophesied over me that I was going to go and preach. I didn't own a suitcase, so I threw everything I had in a box, tied it up, and was ready to go. But it was not time for the effect of that message, because I was not ready. God uses this waiting period between cause and effect to teach us patience and obedience.

Another factor to consider is that we will not always know exactly what the effect is going to be. When Jesus told His followers to "tarry in Jerusalem until they were endued with power from on high," some may have thought, "Man, I'm going to be the high priest here. All of the others are going to be under me." They may have had delusions of grandeur. Out of more than five hundred people who saw Jesus during the forty days between His Resurrection and Ascension, only one hundred and twenty got the message. Only a fourth of them received the "cause" and began to wait on the "effect."

When the effect came, all of them were surprised. No one knew exactly what the manifestation of the Holy Spirit would be. It is useless to try and guess how God is going to bring His Word to pass. When Jesus came, none of the religious leaders recognized Him as the "effect" of the message that had been preached for centuries: Messiah is coming.

They were blind to the truth because they had developed their own preconceived ideas of what the "effect" would be. To accept the true Messiah, they would have to let go of tradition, families, lands and earthly ambitions. Most of them would not pay the price.

I remember a young man at the farm in Mountaindale who was engaged to a pretty, young Puerto Rican girl. He used to go around showing her picture, bragging about how beautiful she was. Then one day, he got a letter from her. The letter said, "Either you come home now, or we are through." I will never forget what that young man did. He was called to preach, and he had just preached on "Count All Things as Loss for Jesus," based on Paul's writings in Philippians 3:8.

He said, "See this girl? I love her and want to marry her. I have been blessed that she would even look at me. But she says if I do not come home this week, we are through. God told me to come here to this farm, to stay here until He tells me to leave. So I must 'count her but loss' for the excellency of the knowledge of Christ Jesus." He dropped her picture on the ground and preached one of the most anointed sermons I have ever heard about casting everything at the foot of the cross. I have never forgotten that.

God later sent him a prettier wife than the one he "gave up," a girl who wanted to serve the Lord with him. Today, they have several children and he is a doctor of theology, one of the leaders in his denomination. God has done much for that man, all because he gave up everything to follow Jesus Christ.

There is a *cause*, and there is an *effect*. In between, there is an *until*. Tarry until you are endued. If we do not expect an "effect," we will not pay any attention to the "cause." Do you fall asleep when you read the Bible? Do you get tired? That happens because the effect is not registered in your mind. Without an effect, we have no incentive to do anything.

If a person knew the world was going to be destroyed, and the only way to survive was to study the Bible, and be able to quote verbatim at least twenty chapters, what would he do? He would study the Bible diligently. Suppose he would be given a million dollars if he read the Bible before midnight. Talk about fast reading! No one would have to prompt him.

Anne was preaching a tremendous message one Sunday morning. It was a beautiful sermon filled with many truths. Yet at 11:45 a.m., I saw some people leaving church. I thought, "Why did they come? It could not have been to receive the message. They are leaving before it is over." Sometimes the last fifteen minutes of a message are the best, particularly when it is a teaching, and all the points lead up to a crucial conclusion. What was the *cause* of those people attending church that morning? Because they left early, they certainly did not receive God's desired *effect.*

We must know *what* we are doing and *why* in order to receive God's best in our Christian walk as well as in our daily activities living in the world. We must decide we are not going to lose this match. We are going to win. The devil will "go down for the count," not us.

We are in a fight with a real enemy, but "the fix is in." That's right, this match is fixed. Two thousand years ago, Jesus got on the cross and winked at the Father, and the Father winked back at Him. The devil did not know what was going on. The fight was won two thousand years ago, but we have to slug it out with our opponent until the end. The devil is not fighting Jesus any longer. He is fighting the Church.

The place where we learn *cause, effect* and *until* is the local church. The church is "the armory of God," the place where the weapons and ammunition are kept, the boot camp where supernatural soldiers are trained.

The Armory of God

The local church is the place we gather to prepare ourselves for war, where the ammunition and equipment are kept. Churches should be like the "tower of David" Solomon wrote about when he compared his beloved's neck to that tower.

Thy neck is like the tower of David builded for an armory, whereon there hang a thousand bucklers, all shields of mighty men.

Song of Solomon 4:4

When we think of an armory, we think of protection. We think of a group of people who have prepared and trained themselves for a specific emergency, to protect the community. At an armory we see vehicles designed for warfare, with armament to use against the enemy, and people in uniform making preparations.

The "ammunition" of God has been deposited in the Church, within us, the people of God—individually and corporately. This ammunition is the power of the Holy Spirit. The local church is the armory where we learn how to develop and use that power. Jeremiah talks about God's armory that was used against the Chaldeans, who were a type of the world.

The Lord hath opened His armory, and hath brought forth the weapons of His indignation: for this is the work of the Lord God of hosts in the land of the Chaldeans.

Jeremiah 15:25

The Church is revealed here as an army waging war against the powers of darkness. We are not to "smoke the peace pipe" or to work out a compromise. When Jesus said to make peace with your enemy on the way to court, He was not talking about the devil (Matthew 5:25)! He was talking about flesh and blood enemies to whom you turn the other cheek (Matthew 5:39).

There is not going to be a reconciliation with the world systems, as man was reconciled to God. In times to come, we must know how to fight, or we are going to be destroyed. That is why we attend church, to learn how to wage war, how to maneuver the buckler, the shield and the sword. We must learn how to duck and when to give ground in order to gain more on another front. Some people get the sword in their hands and want to go out to fight without any preparation, without knowing how to protect themselves. They go out against the enemy, get slapped down, beat up and "stomped" on. They come back bleeding, wounded and discouraged. It is much better to get training in the armory than to face the enemy unprepared. Christians really need to learn discipline.

Once we enlist in God's army, we must submit to God's training program and obey the Holy Spirit so we can do the works of God (James 1:22). We must learn to be obedient to the leadership God has placed over us.

We come into God's armory to learn discipline under the five-fold ministries. In the old Roman gladiator schools, those chosen were trained under a master trainer. He had the right to teach because he had fought in the arena himself. The master gladiator had been bloodied in combat, and had tasted the nearness of death, having faced his adversaries time and time again. He was awarded this honor because of the many victories he had won. He was given certain students that only he alone was permitted to train. Those students learned his style of combat and no other trainer was permitted to assist in their training, lest they become confused in the ring and be destroyed.

There are many today in the spiritual arena of combat, who have had many trainers and are confused because of the different styles and visions, and ultimately they will be destroyed. We must come to the church to be trained, so when our time in the arena comes, we will not be scratching our head, wondering what to do.

In the natural armies of our day, that drill sergeant directing, training and instructing the recruits is "only a man." But he has stripes that tell the recruits that he has earned his position through instruction and submission to a master. Thus he has the authority to give them orders and expect them to do what he says. God's officers also have "stripes," and disregarding them will put us in direct conflict with God Himself.

What good is spiritual power if we don't know how to use it? What good is the sword of the Spirit if we don't know how to swing it? We don't attend church just to sing and shout or worship God. He places us there to learn how to wage war, to be trained in the things of God. We're training to invade the territory of the evil principalities and powers of this world!

Every recruit's training begins in boot camp. A new Christian can go to twenty schools of theology, but if he is not under the covering of the ministry and the Word of God, he is not going to get perfected. We must sit under the governing body that God has established as His government on earth today, which is the five-fold ministry in the local church.

Upon arrival at a military boot camp, raw recruits must take off their "civilian" clothes. When God gives a calling, He starts our preparation by stripping off our death clothes. A whole lot of stuff comes off! Maybe we looked nice when we walked in—we thought we looked very fashionable and distinguished. But now we are going to wear the same "uniform" as others, have the same haircut, and conform to the image portrayed by that branch of the service.

The recruit also loses his independence. When that bugle blows, he doesn't lay there and wonder if he wants to get up or not. We may think that Christians are free and independent people. Not so. We serve one of two masters (Matthew 6:24). When we join the Lord's army, we change masters. There is no neutral ground where we can just do our own thing. We either serve Jesus or satan. If we don't make a choice for Jesus, we serve satan by default.

Jesus is destroying the works of satan, rounding up enemy troops and wiping out his territory—and He's doing it through His Church, His Body. As members of God's army, we need to remember that the battle is not ours, but His.

God's armory is the place to learn how marriages and families are supposed to work according to the Word. If we operate any other way, the enemy will fight us on that ground and knock us out. The armory is the place to learn how to birth sheep into the fold. The Bible says they dance and rejoice in Heaven over one sinner who becomes born again.

Likewise, I say unto you, there is joy in the presence of the angels of God over one sinner that repenteth.

Luke 15:10

The armory is where we learn to love our brothers, to work with them as a unit, a team, and to give a good account of ourselves.

The armory is a hospital we can come back to when we are sick, wounded or depressed. Some Christians have so much pride, they do not want to admit they need prayer. But the armory is where we get assistance. No soldier ever is so perfect that he does not need help sometimes.

I would like to tell everyone that all is wonderful in the Christian life, that a person "has it made" once he is saved. I would like to be able (like some) to preach that the enemy cannot touch the believer, but I must tell the truth from the Word. If there were no testings and trials, the Word of God would not be true.

> *These things I have spoken unto you, that in Me ye might have peace. In the world ye shall have tribulation: but be of good cheer; I have overcome the world.*
>
> John 16:33

Round 9

The Battle Is Not Yours

The battle is not ours, any more than Israel's taking the Promised Land was their battle. They fought, but God won the battles when they used His plans. God said the battle was His (Exodus 14:13-14; Deuteronomy 1:29-30; 2 Chronicles 20:15).

From the beginning, the devil has waged a dirty, no-holds-barred war against God's people. God knows the devil well—that he has no scruples and fights "dirty." We won't destroy the works of a dirty fighter by fighting half-heartedly or in ignorance.

Do you remember the seven sons of Sceva in Acts 19:14-17? These "preacher's boys" thought they could cast out devils by mimicking the actions of God's man—all it got them was the scare of their life, public embarrassment and bruises all over their bodies!

The devil hates God's people, and he'll try anything to stop them—especially if they're doing something for God. From the moment God revealed his plan to bring the Israelites out of Egypt, the fight was on. The devil used the pride of Pharaoh to kill innocent Hebrew babies while trying to strike down God's appointed deliverer, Moses. So Pharoah's heart was so hardened that he refused to free God's people—even when he knew he was fighting against God Himself!

God sent locusts, frogs, lice, and turned water to blood, unleashing ten plagues in all—still Pharoah would not yield. Seeing God's servant work miracles before his eyes, Pharoah refused to obey God's command. Only at this point did God send a death angel into the "midst of Egypt" to take the lives of all the firstborn in the land, human and animal (Exodus 11:4).

God did not start that battle, but He sure ended it! He even arranged for the Israelites to take all of the gold, silver and ornaments that the Egyptians would give them. Some people don't get the message—no matter how many times God deals with them, or how hard He tries to communicate His will to them. Their hearts are hardened. Pharaoh didn't seem to get the message and followed after God's people to destroy them.

The whole scene must have frustrated God. Here was an all-time champion Egyptian "hardhead" following a whole nation of Hebrew hardheads! When the Israelites discovered they had the Red Sea in front and the Egyptian army behind, they fell into hysterical fear and panic because they didn't have confidence in God. They had seen plenty of evidence that God does not need earthly armies, swords or anything else to win His battles.

But the Israelites jumped all over Moses and said, "We knew you'd get us in trouble! Why didn't you leave us alone to be slaves? We had leeks, garlics, and onions, and we ate well. Look what you've done to us. Did you bring us all out here to die?" (Exodus 14:13-14)

God said, *"Hold out your rod and cross the sea on dry ground. I will get honor upon Pharaoh and his hosts, and the Egyptians will know that I am God"* (Exodus 14:16-17).

The same water that parted for the Israelites consumed the Egyptian army. What was the glory of God over the Israelites became the wrath of God over the Egyptians. Too many Christians today try to do God's work without the safety of His glory over them. We will always stumble and fall and be consumed in the battle if we do not have God's glory with us. God often wins a battle through miracles using the natural elements of the earth. One of those battles is described in the Book of Second Chronicles, chapter twenty:

O our God, wilt Thou not judge them? For we have no might against this great company that cometh against us, neither know we what to do; but our eyes are upon Thee.

In verse 12, the Israelites looked at the massive armies of their enemies and said, "God, we do not have the power or the armament. We do not have the strength, the understanding or the knowledge. We do not have a plan and are totally at their mercy." In verse 13, something spiritual happened:

And all Judah stood before the Lord, with their little ones, their wives, and their children.

Where is the best place to put the little ones? In the house of God standing before the Lord, not home watching television or some ungodly video film. The television set is not a good babysitter.

The very next verse shows us it is always good to have a prophet around. The Spirit of the Lord came upon a Levite named Jahaziel, and he spoke from the midst of the congregation:

And he said, Hearken ye, all Judah, and ye inhabitants of Jerusalem, and thou King Jehoshaphat, Thus saith the Lord unto you, Be not afraid nor dismayed by reason of this great multitude; for **the battle is not yours,** *but God's...*

Ye shall not need to fight in this battle: set yourselves, stand ye still, and see the salvation of the Lord with you, O Judah and Jerusalem: fear not, nor be dismayed; to-morrow go out against them: for the Lord will be with you.

                                        2 Chronicles 20:15, 17

The combined armies of three desert nations were coming to drive the Jews out of their promised land. Judah at that time had no army that could fight them off. They confessed their inability to handle the situation and cried out for God to judge their enemies. That's when God told them they did not have to fight. These nations were coming against Jehovah, so He would take care of them. God told Judah to go down against these armies, but not to worry. He even told them where the enemy was and the way he was coming. Some of them may have thought, "Well, Lord, since You are going to do it, would You mind if I stayed home and finished putting in my crops?" But God said, "Get yourselves up tomorrow and go down against them. I want to teach you something." You'll never get the message staying home. You'll have to go the battlefield to learn the lesson!

God uses every testing, trial and circumstance to train us, although He does not instigate all of them. He will use those things to produce more trust and confidence in Him, and a fresh awareness of His love and mercy and power.

The Hebrew children would never have known what it meant to look their enemies in the face and trust God if He had just wiped the enemy out without requiring a step of faith on their part. The same is true for us. For example, we will never be able to understand and comfort others over the loss of a loved one, if we have never been through it.

King Jehoshaphat and God's people began to do what they could do. Jehoshaphat and the people fell on their faces and worshiped God with the Levites and the priests, praising God with loud voices (2 Chronicles 20:18-19). If you cannot win a battle yourself, then begin to worship and praise the Lord and watch Him fight.

The next morning, the king appointed singers to go before the army, praising the beauty of God's holiness. They sang: *"Praise the Lord; for his mercy endureth for ever"* (Psalm 136:1). As they began to sing and praise the Lord, the Bible says that God set "ambushments" against the enemy (2 Chronicles 20:20-22).

God often uses "ambushments" to confound His enemies. Basically, it means He turned them against one another. They were so busy fighting among themselves that they ignored Judah. Moab and Ammon turned on those from Mount Seir (the Edomites), and when they had "made an end" of them, every one helped to destroy another (2 Chronicles 20:23).

I want you to notice that the singers the king appointed were holy singers. They were quite different from those who sing the songs of satan. I have seen a number of supposedly saved entertainers get "knocked out in the ring" because they were not willing to totally come out of the world to sing for the Lord. When we get saved, our talent needs to "get saved" too.

I have heard all the excuses, "You have to go out where the people are. I can go out there and witness to the sinner. I can sing, and my testimony will reach those who are really hurting."

Many of these entertainers were wiped out on drugs, in the hospital, or almost dead, when God reached down and saved them. At first everything was for the glory of God. They surrendered their time, their talents and their careers. What did they have to lose? Then, after a time, their tune changed. "Well, after all, God gave me this talent, and I can use it for Him. I can witness in front of my old friends so we can reach them." I have never seen it work yet. You can't serve two masters.

These singers of Jehoshaphat's were singing unto the Lord! They were "the sacrificial lambs," out in front of the army, not safe behind the lines. They did not have swords, shields or armament. All they had were their voices and a praise chorus written by King David. Even today, anointed praisers and worshipers are the front line troops in the army of God.

A modern-day "ambushment" by God happened in the war against Iraq. Back in the seventies, the Arab oil-producing nations had the Western world by the throat. Do you remember the oil cartel? Do you remember gasoline shortages and oil prices? For some "unknown reason," the Islamic nations that had banded together to bring the Christian world to its knees began to turn on one another. Suddenly, they began fighting among themselves. Iraq went to war with Iran, and there was no harmony in the Islamic world. Like the Tower of Babel, a lot of confusion resulted. In the meantime, the Western nations, and especially the United States, accumulated more oil and gas than before.

The confusion of Islam continued until Iraq went to war against Kuwait, and the Saudi royal family actually had to make an alliance with the West to save themselves. Finally, a predominently American task force took on Iraq in direct conflict, with almost no casualties—a miracle considering the number of troops involved.

That happened because Christians got in unity and prayed (Matthew 18:19-20).

If America is to survive, we need to continue to pray for this country. God will tolerate a system that says "in God we trust," even if we are not operating in His perfect will. But He will not tolerate a nation that says, "There is no God." He gave the Soviet Union seventy years of mercy, then made them an open display of shame. He tore down the walls of godless communism until it almost looks as though Europe is going back into an era of many small nations, divided by race and culture.

If America and other great Western nations do not turn themselves around and look at God's statutes, they are going to reap a whirlwind of devastation. I will say it again and again. The richest nations on earth could become the poorest overnight. God is not going to change His laws for any man or nation. He has devised a plan for whatever enemy has come against you. It might not look like a plan of war. Who would call a march around a city a battleplan? Who would consider going out singing praises as warfare?

God has a plan for every nation on earth—He is looking for obedient people with the courage to carry out these plans. God had the Israelites march around Jericho six days, then seven times on the seventh day. They blew trumpets and shouted (Joshua 6:20). In Joshua 6:2, God told Joshua He had given the city, its king, and its mighty men of valor into his hand. Before they got to the city, the Lord had a plan, the battle was already won. If you want to win in the Kingdom of God, the plan must be God's. If you want the battle to be His, the plan must be His. If you are walking according to His purpose, will and plan, then He already has provided protection.

In our early days, one of our deacons said, "Brother John, if a business was run the way you run this church, it would be bankrupt!" Another businessman turned to this brother and said, "I wish my business was in as good of shape as this church. We have no unpaid bills and no indebtedness. It seems to me that God is in control of this church."

All we did was ask God what to do next. We can do business in the world the same way and not go bankrupt, by simply obeying God's laws of sowing and reaping. We did not borrow money or go through the world's systems. We were building the church at the time, and would get the bills for the week on Friday. On Sunday, we would bring the bills before the Lord and say, "Here they are." We would begin to worship, and somehow all of the bills got paid. We had no money, but every week, the bills were taken care of. God had said, "Don't go to the arm of the flesh. I am going to provide."

We believed it, and He did it! God has continued to pay our bills, too. That was His battle plan for us, and we received it. If we had gotten a loan from the world for a mortgage, we would have ended up paying back many times the value of the loan.

We serve a *supernatural* God. It's hard to put supernatural things in a box! The Bible says that God "confounded" the enemy and slew them. They became like drunken people, could not comprehend what was going on, and staggered around. Another time, He blinded His enemies and threw down "great stones" on them (Joshua 10:11). It does not say the angels did it: God threw them, slaying more than Israel had with the sword. God is a real "sharpshooter."

Modern military experts think they have guidance systems down to a science now. They can press a button, and a weapon can strike a target thousands of miles away. But God threw large stones on the enemy from the heavens with pinpoint accuracy, missing all of His own people!

If some other nation loosed nuclear weapons at this country, God's people could be like the Hebrew children in the fiery furnace. If we are in unity and in the right place in God, we could be praising God and rejoicing while death rained down all around us, just like the Israelites in Egypt.

Once God thundered over the Philistines and threw them into confusion (1 Samuel 7:10). When Hezekiah was king of Judah, God sent an angel to save Judah from Assyria. Hezekiah did not have to do anything (2 Chronicles 32:21).

As we read all of these Old Testament incidents about Israel and Judah in war, we discover three patterns for spiritual warfare:

1 - God has the plan all prepared, and He always wins the battle.

2 - We must walk according to His purpose and do our part, whether it is to fight, sing, march or pray.

3 - God's plan and tactics are not always the same. Each battle requires finding out what God wants us to do in each circumstance and doing it. Sometimes, our only job is to "clean up the mess."

The ten steps of spiritual warfare (given in a previous chapter) help us get to a place where we can be obedient when God gives us His plan. Once we have that, all we have to do is be strong and courageous.

Round 10

Be Strong and Courageous

Joshua was the perfect example of a leader called of God to be strong and courageous. Joshua began right, walked right, and ended right. His life can help us to see what God means by "strong and courageous."

Joshua served Moses for years, just as Elisha served Elijah. If you want to find out who God will use next, look for the one who is serving. Scan the crowd for the one who is always helping others and reaching out to give of himself. Don't look for the one who doesn't show compassion or concern, and who doesn't give of himself. Pass right over the one who is proud, thinking he should be waited on. God rewards faithfulness. Look at God's reward to Joshua for his faithfulness to Moses:

There shall not any man be able to stand before thee all the days of thy life: as I was with Moses, so I will be with thee: I will not fail thee, nor forsake thee.

Be strong and of a good courage: for unto this people shalt thou divide for an inheritance the land which I sware unto their fathers to give them.

Only be thou strong and very courageous, that thou mayest observe to do according to all the law, which Moses, my servant, commanded thee: turn not from it to the right hand or to the left, that thou mayest prosper whithersoever thou goest...

Have I not commanded thee? **Be strong and of a good courage;** *be not afraid, neither be thou dismayed: for the Lord thy God is with thee whithersoever thou goest...*

Whosoever he is that doth rebel against thy command-ment, and will not hearken unto thy words in all that thou commandest him, he shall be put to death: only **be strong and of good courage.**

Joshua 1:6-7, 9, 18

Why did God want Joshua to be strong and very courageous? Joshua had to be totally obedient—he couldn't af-ford to veer off to the left or right of God's commands. God wanted Joshua to walk in obedience so he would finish God's plan to get Israel into the Promised Land, and so that Joshua himself might prosper.

God's order, *be strong and of good courage,* was so impor-tant that the Lord repeated the phrase four times in His first in-struction to Joshua. Any time God repeats something, we had better pay attention!

Moses had used the same phrase in his farewell speech—as a word from the Lord—once to the Israelites and twice to Joshua. Within just a few days' time, Joshua heard *"be strong and courageous"* seven times (Deuteronomy 31:6, 7, 23).

The four times God said it directly to Joshua reveals four different reasons to be strong.

Be Strong for the Sake of the People

God was saying, "Joshua, be strong for the sake of the people" (Joshua 1:6).

Leaders need to make strong stands so that their followers will see their strength and be able to do the same. Weak leaders make weak followers. Even worse, a strong but frustrated follower may be tempted to slip into an "Absalom spirit" and try to take over.

In 1 Peter 5:3, elders are exhorted to take the oversight of the flock, not forcefully, not for money, not as "lording" it over them, but as examples. They need to be strong and not ask anyone else to do what they would not do. When you accept leadership in any capacity, your responsibility increases along with the authority. Leaders are supposed to *lead*. Spiritual warfare requires direction. God's army has generals, captains, lieutenants, sergeants and privates.

Those who box in the ring must have trainers and helpers. Soldiers must have back-up support available. We may give these examples different names or titles, but the principle remains: leaders must lead.

Elders and deacons, as well as those in the ministry of helps, must set an example for the people. Those callings were established to serve the people. The first deacons were literally selected to wait on tables (Acts 6:1-7), but they were still on the front lines of warfare. Look at what happened to Stephen. The first Christian martyr was a deacon—a table waiter—not an apostle, prophet or pastor.

In some churches, deacons seem to think they are masters, not servants. Some deacon boards tell their pastor what to do, or even choose the pastors—it's no wonder these churches stay in chaos. Our local churches will never have the stability God intended until they adopt the format God intended. If there are deacons in a church who are not willing to serve, if they are not the first to put up their hands when volunteers are needed, something is wrong. Remember: the chronological age of the deacons does not matter. Paul wrote Timothy not to let his youth be despised, but to be **an example** to the believers in conversation, in love, in spirit, in faith and in purity (1 Timothy 4:12).

Be Strong for Your Own Sake

Secondly, God told Joshua to be strong and courageous for his own sake. A show of strength for the people's sake is not enough. A leader must do what he is supposed to do in order to prosper. Being **strong** means being disciplined in both body and soul, keeping every area of your life under authority—including your time.

Paul said he must keep his body under authority, lest he "become a castaway" after preaching to others. We must practice what we preach (1 Corinthians 9:27).

God wants those who serve Him to succeed and prosper. He does not delight in failure because He does not fail, and we are made in His image. We are supposed to be prosperous and successful, but we have to follow His principles (keep His commandments) in order for that to happen.

Be Strong for the Lord's Sake

The Lord's third admonition to be strong and courageous was for His own sake. Eliminate fear and dismay for the Lord thy God is with thee. God is always pleased when our trust and confidence is in Him instead of people or ourselves. Cain brought sacrifices and offerings. Cain was "religious," but God was not pleased. Cain pleased himself at the cost of displeasing God. There are a lot of religious "events" going on today that please the people and ministers, but they aren't pleasing God.

It is easy for us to look good when we are in public. But are we strong and courageous in private? How do we treat our husbands and wives behind closed doors? God is even interested in what we eat and drink. He does not like for mankind to drink polluted waters, breathe impure air, or eat foods that are contaminated with chemicals. Man has brought all of this on himself. The world is walking under the curses, not the blessings, because of its attitude toward God.

God is interested in our conduct with one another because our private lives reveal our true attitudes about God's commandments. However, His primary interest is in our relationship with Him.

But seek ye first the Kingdom of God, and His righteousness; and all these things shall be added unto you.

Matthew 6:33

Be Strong Because of the Enemy

The fourth reason Joshua was to be strong and of good courage was because of the enemy—an enemy who wants to destroy God's leaders and believers. The devil constantly plots and schemes to bring division and chaos into the Body of Christ. If you are doing anything for God, there is a devil who wants to get you.

If you are not doing anything, you are probably "safe"—the devil has you where he wants you. He doesn't have to search for a way to knock you out—you have already laid down and rolled over for him. If you are living far below your Christian responsibilities not using your authority in Jesus, you will not prosper.

We must stand against the rebels who allow satan to use them to help destroy the work of God. We must learn to recognize and deal with those who come as wolves in sheep's clothing, the people the enemy uses to bring strife and devastation into a church. Sometimes they sit right next to us and whisper in our ear. They disrupt and disturb—they'll do almost anything to steal the Word of God from the hearts of His people.

When God told Joshua to be **strong**, He wanted him to be strong spiritually, physically and mentally. **Strong** means to be firm, durable, powerful, vigorously effective, intense in degree or quality, and even "strong in wealth."

God also told Joshua to be courageous. To be **courageous** means to venture forth, to persevere, to withstand danger, fear,

or difficulty, to be firm and tenacious and to have stubborn per-
sistence. It means to have firmness of mind and will—even in
the face of extreme difficulty or danger. A few years ago, this
quality of being strong and courageous was summed up in the
slogan, "having the right stuff."

It takes training and practice to be strong and courageous.
Joshua spent years waiting on Moses and learning to be a servant before he moved into leadership. Joshua also developed a
relationship with God during that time. When Moses left the
tent or tabernacle, the Bible says that Joshua stayed behind (Exodus 33:11). Now he wasn't simply staying behind in an empty
tent, he was staying behind *in the presence of God Almighty.*
Joshua got to know His Commander-in-Chief in the spirit
before he went into the field of battle leading Israel to victory
over Jericho (Joshua 5:14).

Be Strong by Eliminating Weaknesses

When we set out to firm up our physical bodies, we find our
weak places and work on them to build consistent muscle tone
and development. It is no different in the spirit. Find your weak
areas and exercise them if you want to be a "Joshua." Strength
comes from exercise. Courage comes as we get to know our
Commander-in-Chief.

Are you weak in prayer? Set a realistic prayer schedule to
"firm up" that area. Ninety-eight percent of the Church does not
pray enough. Prayer is the "granddaddy" of all spiritual exer-
cises, the "bench-press" of the Christian "body-building" program. Find every occasion to pray. When you get up in the
morning, pray first before doing anything else. When you go to
bed at night, let prayer be the last thing you do. The more you
pray, the stronger you get.

Are you weak in Bible study? Then make a "dinner appointment" each day to feed your spirit by reading God's Word. Most
of us have to make ourselves exercise and eat right, but it is

worth it. How much more valuable will it be to exercise and refuel in Bible study and prayer?

Are you weak in giving? Map out a budget that includes tithes and the best offerings possible. Do without some things that are not necessities in order to give more. Exercise your giving so that you will become strong in that area and prosper. If you keep that ten percent for bills, you are robbing yourself too, not just God. Practice giving. The more you give, the easier it gets.

Are you weak in church attendance? This may be the easiest place to begin your spiritual exercise. Beginning body-builders are advised to begin with something easy that does not strain their muscles. Going to church is the easiest way to start. There are others to pray with, the anointing to lift you up, teaching and preaching from God's Word, and an opportunity to exercise your giving.

Are you weak in your family structure? Plan to spend more time with your spouse and your children. Determine to really listen to what they are saying. Try at least once a week to find something you can do for them that they need or desire, something that will build a relationship, to show them you really do care.

Are you weak in your work habits? Do you put in a good day's work? Or do you sneak off the job or skimp a little here and there on your job duties? Do you give your employer the best that's in you to the glory of God?

Here are some other areas of the spirit-man we may be weak in:

1 - *Mercy*, loving your neighbors.

2 - *Forgiveness*, patience and longsuffering.

3 - Other *fruits of the spirit* (Galatians 5:22-23).

4 - *Serving others*.

5 - *Seeking the will of God*.

Some may be thinking, "But all of those things are hard work." All exercise is work in the beginning. Only after we have gotten strong in most areas does it become easy. Runners talk about "getting their second wind." That only comes after we run until it hurts, until we think we cannot run anymore.

Being strong and courageous does not come without sacrifice. Being a champion boxer in the realm of the spirit and in the image of your Father will not happen easily. There is a saying today that sums this up: "No pain, no gain." It is easy to exercise when we really do not need it, but it does the most good when we really need it—when it hurts.

We will never get strong simply by wishing. It is easy to begin, but the hard part is continuing. We all start out on these "programs" of physical training with a lot of enthusiasm and energy. However, about the second or third week of getting up an hour early to go jogging, it becomes very, very hard. But once it becomes a habit, you have to do it or you don't feel good.

The flesh gives up quickly. We become weary in well-doing (Galatians 6:9). So stay at it. The rewards are certainly worth it. Conduct produces character, and character produces power. Once we are trained, strong and courageous, we can learn the principles of warfare.

Round 11

Principles of War: Fight to Win

I learned to fight as a young boy. I even liked to fight, but I was not bent on suicide. I learned it didn't pay to fight with someone bigger. I wanted to be victorious, I liked to win.

I belonged to a gang in my neighborhood where I grew up. When two of us were ready to fight, one of us would say to the other, "Give me a fair one." That meant, "Don't pull no guns, knives, sticks, or other weapons." The other one would say, "Yeah! I'll give you a fair one." That meant we were going to fight with fists, feet or teeth—but no weapons. The fights may have started out that way, but none of them ever ended up that way! Before it was over, the fight would get awfully dirty. I never knew how to give anyone a "fair one" in the world. We thought if we did that, we would end up the guaranteed loser because the other guy would find some way to "do us in." I learned to be tricky in order to win, because my opponent was not playing games. He was setting out to hurt me.

When I became a Christian, I discovered that I couldn't give the devil "a fair one." We shouldn't give him any breaks. When he is down, "stomp" him! Believe me, when we are down, he will trample on us. We must learn every way we can to bring down the enemy.

Many churches and Christians have been fooled into thinking the devil is going to give them "a fair one." They've forgotten what the Bible calls this "fair" being: the father of lies! He does not fight fair. He wants to destroy your very soul, to get you any way he can: through your spouse, your friends and neighbors, or your family members.

The *main* principle to remember when going into warfare is *fight to win*. Vietnam was a disaster, a travesty for the United States: we did not go into it to win. America went into Vietnam as a "police action," and the top government officials never turned the military loose to win.

There is a way to win and a way to lose. Most of the time, it's no accident that we lose. First, we have to *give up* in our minds to prepare ourselves to lose.

No one "accidentally" falls away from God. They have to turn away from Him toward something else they love more. Men slide backwards and go away from God because they want to.

Many scriptures talk about warfare in one way or another. It does not matter how much we speak in tongues or engage in church activities, we must know the Word of God, or we will not be successful in our spiritual lives. You must have a good understanding of the Word in order to do battle.

The Bible is the "blueprint," the architect's drawing of the edifice called the Church. We must look at the blueprints to make sure everything is according to specification, from the first to the last day of construction. There are inspectors who come by periodically to make sure the building is up to standards. In the spiritual world, the Holy Spirit is the Inspector. Sometimes He must tell us to tear things down and start over.

Any time we build something at Rock Church, there is an inspector who comes by and checks out the construction. Sometimes it's hard not to get frustrated with him. We think we've followed the blueprint as carefully as possible, but he may say, "No, you have to put in more steel." Of course, that costs thousands of dollars more, but it has to be done according to the specifications.

There is an enemy who makes it as difficult as possible for us to build, tears down things behind your back, and sneers at you for even trying to build. We need to know as much about him as possible.

Know Your Enemy

The *second* principle of war is: *Know your opponent.*

Our adversary is out to destroy us, and he is a tyrant who cares nothing about fair play, "democratic principles," mercy or understanding. We can see this by the characteristics of those who rule in an ungodly way. Earthly tyrants tried to destroy the Church throughout history, from the early Roman emperors to Hitler. The Nazis tried to wipe out all the Jews in their territory, and the true Church as well. Only those who agreed with the state and its tyrannical aims were not bothered.

Our adversary is a frustrated, bad-tempered and angry enemy. He is frustrated because he has never been able to get the best of God. He has always lost his major endeavors. He wins the minor battles that people and nations give to him, but God's plan goes "marching on."

Satan already knows that he is a defeated foe, and he knows his final destination. He has been reading it in the Book of Revelation and hearing it talked about for the past two thousand years. All he can hope to do is take as many people created in the image of God with him as he can.

Any being rash enough to think he could challenge God has to have a certain amount of insanity about him, to say nothing of a colossal, stupendous ego. Satan wants to be God, to rule in our lives and in the world, to be worshiped. Every time I hear a brother say, "I wrestled with God last night," I really have a good chuckle over this and I always watch to see if he limps when he walks away.

The Word of God says that satan is the "father of lies" (John 8:44). From the days of Adam and Eve in the Garden of Eden, our enemy has lied. He lied to them, and he has lied to every man since. His troops whisper lies in your ears. The higher-level demons work to propagate lies about God, creation, the origin of man, and what is right and wrong through various "world" systems.

All philosophies, religions, political systems, economic theories, educational philosophies and systems, and entertainment fields that are not based on the Word of God are based on the lies of satan. All of them are false, because he is false. All of them are designed to hurt, destroy or steal from man.

Satan may be the instigator, originator and overseer of those systems, but he does not own the **earth**. There are many scriptures that show God never relinquished ownership of the planet, but only gave man the right to rule over it as a steward (Genesis 1:26; Psalm 24:1; Isaiah 66:1).

The enemy is the master of dirty tricks. He plays to all the "human" weaknesses. He attempts to use our flesh, the "old man," to trip us up. He works extra hard to turn even our strengths into weaknesses.

The devil tries to keep us from following through on the purpose that God has for our lives. He may cause us to to marry too soon or become involved with addictions, or all kinds of activities that keep us "living on the edge," flirting with death.

If the enemy cannot trip us up, he tries to push us in the wrong direction. What looks like the opportunity of a lifetime may be satan's attempt to pull us away or distract us from the real purpose of God. For example, how many people called to be good Christian administrators and stewards over large works for God have been sidetracked into the world's business system?

When we enter a fight, we must go all-out to win. To do that, we must know our opponent, his weak and strong points. Then we need to be prepared. Once we are trained and strengthened to fight, we must go out to win. The opponent's strong points are his dirty tricks, and his weak points are that he has already lost every battle with God and will lose the ultimate battle with the Church.

Have the Spirit of a Winner

The *third* principle of winning a war is that we must have *"the spirit of a winner."* We must believe we have a righteous cause important enough to merit the investment of our whole life and heart. We must be constantly vigilant, watching the enemy's tactics. And we must persevere and stick with the battle until we win.

Most Christians believe they have a "righteous cause," but few of us give ourselves totally to that cause. Our flesh may be invested in the enemy's domain, causing breaches or broken down places in our walls. The more we get involved in things of the world, the weaker our defenses become.

Being vigilant involves watching our own defenses as well as the tactics, traps and tricks of the enemy. In Great Britain during World War II, air raid wardens and plane spotters saved many lives. In the United States, we also used these important volunteers to watch for the enemy—especially in the coastal areas and around strategic military sites.

Spend as much time as possible in prayer and communion with the Holy Spirit so you will be able to be vigilant toward the enemy. Part of the Holy Spirit's role is to be the Watchman for us. If we will listen, He will warn us of things to come, of "punches" the enemy is about to throw. He will trigger an agitation in our spirits, or "lift our peace" about certain things—that is a sure warning that something is wrong (James 3:17).

The Holy Spirit protects our perimeters, but all His knowledge and wisdom will do us no good if we cannot hear Him. It is through prayer and our careful listening that He builds us up so that we can stand the tests that come our way. He backs us up in battle, and His power is ours to wield against the enemy if we operate in faith.

Tests are not always attacks of the enemy, they're sometimes early trials of strength to prepare us *before* we are attacked. Soldiers are put through obstacle courses to test and increase their strength, stamina, and their ability to listen and obey orders. These obstacle courses let others see if they have the hearts of winners. Without these tests and the training they provide, the soldiers would get hurt easily, stumble and fall in weakness, or give up in self-pity.

There are always some people who would rather spend the war in the brig than obey orders and fight. Some Christians are like that, too. We need to understand that God is building us up through all these battles and skirmishes.

God does not take short cuts. He builds everything to last. He is using us as lively (living) stones to build His Son a Body that He will not be ashamed to Head (1 Peter 2:5). God is the Master Architect who trims and shapes us, and then polishes us according to His blueprint. He chooses us first, then He begins to trim us to fit. Finally, after the rough chiseling and fine cutting, He begins to smooth us out with fine sandpaper so we will be able to reflect His glory.

A man with the spirit of a winner wants to be cleaned up, trained and corrected. He knows his spiritual progress and well-being in the natural depend on his forward movement with God. He knows whatever God does is for his benefit, to help him fulfill God's purpose and plan for his life.

We will not always like God's dealings—sometimes we'll even think they are attacks from the enemy. We need to find out *who* is doing *what* for what *reason* before we go into battle. If it's the enemy, we need to fight it. If it is God chiseling, sandpapering or polishing, the best thing to do is yield to the work of the Holy Spirit and get it over with.

If God is doing it, you can be certain the test or trial will *not* destroy, or steal any good thing from you. Things that offend your pride may be God trying to get you to give it up. The important thing is to stay in close fellowship with God so you can discern the origin of those things.

The entire eleventh chapter of Hebrews recalls God's heroes and heroines who have had the spirit of a winner. When the battle is raging against you, look back at that chapter and see those people who survived much worse than you are going through.

They were human. They faced the same kinds of temptation, trials and tests you are facing today. Some actually lost their lives or were in danger of doing so. They faced challenges on every hand and had to fight the enemy for their very lives, yet they all finished the course God had set for them.

In addition, Hebrews 12:1 says we are "compassed about" with a "great cloud of witnesses"; those are the saints who have already been through what we are experiencing. Only a few of them are mentioned by name in that chapter, but countless millions have successfully passed the fire of testings and trials to victory.

Some of these people turned entire nations around. We have more advantages and live more abundantly than they ever did. We have the Holy Spirit *within* us; they did not. If you are a good soldier with a heart to win, then you must be ready to endure hardness and difficulty.

Make up your mind to fight to win, because the battle goes on and will continue until Jesus returns. In fact, the warfare is "heating up" in our day as the enemy sees how short his time has become.

Round 12

The Enemy Without

Christians today are in the same position as the Israelites who were given the land of Canaan. God promised it to them through one man: Abraham. But when God sent Moses to bring the Hebrew nation out of Egypt and to possess the Promised Land, they had grown to "a great company." But they did not yet have the hearts of winners.

They did not trust God totally. They really did not know Him, except as the "God of Abraham, Isaac, and Jacob." They did not know Him personally. When they got to the edge of the Promised Land, they didn't realize it was already theirs. They let fear conquer them. They said, "Those people are too great for us, making us feel like grasshoppers. They'll massacre us. We can't fight them. Moses, what have you gotten us into now?" Instead of saying, "God gave this land to us. The battle is His. If He says take it, we can take it," they wanted to kill Moses, Joshua and Caleb.

Many Christians today are doing the same thing. They look at the world's system and the masses of people who have the seed of satan in them and say, "They make us look like grasshoppers. We cannot take this. We had better find some place to sit and hide until Jesus comes and takes us out of here." They even get mad and "throw stones" at those who teach spiritual warfare.

Canaan's wealth of natural resources were promised to God's children. So today, the natural resources of the earth are here for His people, not for satan's "seed," but the devil wants us to believe that being poor is holy. Why would God give all of the gold, silver, and the "cattle on a thousand hills" to the devil and his people? The devil is defeated, but the Church has let him take her inheritance. In the Middle Ages, the church establishment was wealthy, but they wanted to spend their wealth on their own lusts (James 4:3). That system was brought down. Even with wrong motives, wrong doctrines, wrong behavior and wrong attitudes, they upheld the name of Jesus, so God's mercy extended over the church of that period for about a thousand years.

God loved His children who were trapped in that corrupt religious system, and the prayers of those true saints helped preserve it, just as the prayers of today's saints can preserve the United States. This nation has been the one to uphold the name of Jesus for more than two hundred years.

The Knockout That Won the Victory

There was a time when satan thought he had won. Jesus, in accordance with God's battle plan, allowed Himself to be knocked down, but what seemed to be a knockout punch from the devil was really the final knockout by Jesus.

The devil and all of his troops had a field day when Jesus hung on the cross and said, *It is finished* (John 19:30). They misunderstood what He meant. They thought the battle was finished, and they had won. The devil probably bragged, "I may not have won in the garden of Eden, at the Tower of Babel, or at Sodom and Gomorrah. I may not have won in Bethlehem when Herod killed the babies, but I have won now! We heard Jesus admit it, we heard Him say it's finished. We won!"

He probably shook his fist at God and said, "You sent Adam and Eve, and I dealt with them and their children. You had to cleanse the earth of them, except one family, and all of them were not perfectly righteous. You scattered Noah's children around the world, and divided the earth (Genesis 10:25) to hinder me, but I dealt with them. But You would not give up. You kept on with Israel, and I dealt with them. You sent prophet after prophet, but I had them martyred, and the people sent into exile. You brought them back into this land, and I have dealt with them. Now You actually sent Your Son, and I have dealt with Him. You have lost, God. There is nothing else You can do. Everything You prophesied through the centuries has come to nothing. I am bringing it to an end now, because I have Your Son on the cross. He is knocked down, and I am counting."

The disciples and other followers of Jesus looked at Jesus on the cross and backed away. They heard what He had said, and now they watched Him die. They were very discouraged, thinking that the devil had won the final victory. The demons rejoiced as Jesus hung on the cross, bleeding from His hands, feet and side, and from the crown of thorns on His head.

Then the heavens began to cloud over until there was no light except for the lightning that raced across the sky. The devil thought it was the final curtain, the end of the age-long warfare. This was the center stage of the universe. Demons danced around the cross, enjoying Jesus' suffering while wicked people mocked, cursed and spat on Him, as He hung there and said, "*It is finished.*" The entire universe rocked and shook because of the words of the Lamb of God.

Every prophet and every man and woman of God from the beginning of time was on the "balcony" of Heaven watching this climax of the War of the Ages. The war was finished on the cross (Colossians 2:14-15), but satan had the wrong idea about who won.

The angels understood, the great cloud of witnesses understood, the Father and the Holy Spirit understood what Jesus meant by His words. The victory was God's. He had won the bout by His own Son—Jesus (Isaiah 63:5). God was still the Champion.

Jesus did not stay down for the count. He rose from the dead on the third day in total victory! Satan still did not give up, and stubbornly refused to admit that he had lost. He set out to continue his rebellion. First, he lost to God the Father without striking a blow. Then, in a hopeless battle with God's Son, when he finally got to strike a blow, it resulted in an eternal knockout punch to his own head! Now, he's fighting the Bride of Christ— the Church. He immediately tried to kill the Church in those early days, but he did not succeed and never will.

Since the Day of Pentecost, the Church has been the Champion's representative. It is not actually a true boxing bout because the adversary is already defeated. We are sparring partners, keeping him busy until the real Champion returns to put the challenger where he can do no more damage.

Seven Enemies Without: Driving out the "Ites"

The Church in each generation is to possess the land that God has already given us on this earth—though our eternal home is in Heaven. The Israelites had a natural land given them by God as well as a heavenly one. God will take care of our heavenly home, but it is up to us to take over the earthly one.

The enemies of God who tried to keep the Israelites out of their Promised Land are described in Deuteronomy 7:1-5. The Israelites had to face seven enemy tribes: the **Hittites, Girgashites, Hivites, Amorites, Canaanites, Perizzites and Jebusites.**

These tribes who occupied the Promised Land are a spiritual picture of our enemies today. The **Hittites,** the strongest of these tribes, built an empire that *generated fear.* In their heyday, they took on Babylon, Egypt and Assyria. At the time of the conquest, they were mostly to the north of the Israelites' Promised Land.

The Hittites of Canaan are thought to have been early migrants from the south part of the Canaan empire. They are called "the sons of Heth." They were fierce enemies that brought fear.

Fear is the first enemy humans have to face. Christians are not immune from it; in fact, fear is one of our strongest enemies. There are all kinds of fear, so many kinds that the world has a name for them: *phobias*.

Before Jesus came into my heart, I used to roam the streets in confusion with nowhere to go. Fear can make a man's thinking go wrong. Three fears hinder God's people from taking their land: the fear of man, the fear of the unknown and the fear of tomorrow.

Israel feared the Hittites—even when God was on their side and had promised them **all the land of the Hittites** (Joshua 1:4). We should have no fear of the enemy of the Church today. Fear breaks down the human spirit and makes a way for sin in the heart.

Secondly, the **Girgashites**, the earthy people, were always involved in *the things of the flesh*. They lived for their own pleasure. This is a problem with many Christians today. The Girgashites are a symbol of the flesh or body.

Jesus said that if we would follow Him, we must lay down our lives, which means everything we are or possess (Matthew 16:24, 28). Paul wrote about keeping his body under subjection (1 Corinthians 9:27).

Fleshly people get "in the flesh" and grumble, complain, criticize and gossip. They always put down the things of God; they are self-righteous and ready to criticize any move of God, whether it is praising, dancing or prophesying.

Third on the list are the **Amorites**, a people full of *pride, ego* and *self-exaltation*. We must put down our pride to follow Jesus. There are churches that are prideful, believing they have the only truth. If other churches do not preach it exactly as they do, they think those churches don't know Jesus. They get puffed up thinking they are the only ones going to Heaven.

The Israelites had to conquer two Amorite kings before they got to the Promised Land—Sihon of Heshbon and Og of Bashan. This was the first stage in taking the land before crossing the Jordan River at Jericho (Deuteronomy 3:1-13). Christians have to conquer the tyrants of pride and arrogance before they can cross their "Jordan."

Fourthly, there were the **Canaanites**, the descendants of Ham. Canaan symbolizes idolatry, *the sin of putting something ahead of or in place of God.* The golden calf idol that Israel kept returning to over the centuries was a Canaanite idol that stood for Baal.

"Golden calves" in our lives can be many things, even our spouse or children. In America, it can be a career, a job, worldly possessions or personal ambition. Many Christians try to straddle the fence like Israel did. They want to be known as God's people, yet worship the form of some golden idol.

Fifthly, the Israelites faced **Perizzites**, who lived outside of the walled cities. The Perizzites were the "hippies" of their time. Their name means *inhabitants of the open country.* Their problem was independence, another name for self-will and rebellion. They did not want anyone telling them what to do— they wanted to "do their own thing." That is a delusion. We never do things "our" way. It is always either God's way or the devil's way.

The "Perizzites" we fight today are "self" tendencies: *self-will, self-focus, self-awareness,* even *self-pity.* The Perizzites represent all the things that cause us to think we are the center of our lives and not God. Their name sounds like "parasites," and that is what these are—parasites on the Body of Christ.

The Perizzites were "squatters." They were always camping on someone else's turf with their hands out, begging. These people do not know the same rules apply to them as to everyone else. They are too slothful to go out into the field and be productive. Laziness, like stealing, is a sin.

The sixth group, the **Hivites**, thought small and lived in small encampments, *having no vision.* They thought they could not do it, so they never did. The Hivites represent people with a narrow vision who always want to stay small. God wants to expand and increase us, He wants to keep giving us a greater vision of His will for us.

Finally, there were the **Jebusites**. Full of *self-hatred and self-rejection*, they were always putting themselves and their ancestors down. They thought they could not accomplish anything. They were their own worst enemy.

These seven tribes symbolize the "ites" that must be driven out of our lives: fear, the flesh, pride, elevating things or people above God, ego or "self-exhaltation," lack of vision, and self-rejection or self-hatred. If we put all those things together, we have a picture of the basic ways the enemy comes at us individually. These are the "tribes" we must chase out of our territories today.

Scattering the Enemy

Israel never drove the enemy completely out of the land. Some of them became part of Israel, such as "Uriah the Hittite," whose wife Bathsheba became David's downfall. Because all these tribes were not wiped out as God had said, they caused Israel to fall into idolatry and brought about her fall.

But if ye will not drive out the inhabitants of the land from before you; then it shall come to pass, that those which ye let remain of them shall be pricks in your eyes, and thorns in your sides, and shall vex you in the land wherein ye dwell.

Numbers 33:55

When we cross the Jordan into our land of promise, the land of plenty, the land of power and joy, the land of prosperity, then

God begins to say, "Ye shall drive out all the inhabitants of the land before you."

When we were born again, we took the first step in a lifelong process of taking the territory God has for us. We "crossed the Jordan" when we were baptized in water. The battle begins when you get saved. Then we must chase out the old inhabitants we have been "hobnobbing" with all our lives; those little habits and pleasures that are ungodly and so hard to give up.

God did not say to compromise or ease the "ites" out, or deal with them. It does not matter if your particular "ite" is dealing dope, cheating on your husband or wife, or cheating on your income tax: drive it out! Do not ignore it and hope it will leave. If you have old pictures of yourself doing ungodly things, if you have ungodly record albums, cassettes or videos, get rid of them. Get rid of anything that reminds you of the "dead body" that used to be you.

These are enemies. The "tribes" that inhabit your promised land endanger your soul and spirit. God wants the enemies driven out, first in us, then in the Church corporately, then in the world. He cannot do much with the world until the Church gets straightened out.

If God's people have "Girgashites, Amorites, and Jebusites," the enemy is still within. We must begin destroying the enemy in the things closest to home.

Giants in the Land

In addition to all of the "ites," the Israelites also faced giants. Giants are mentioned in the Bible by different names: the sons of the *Anakim* (they scared ten of the twelve spies and caused Israel to wander in the wilderness for a generation, Deuteronomy 1:28); the *Zuzim* or the *Zamzummins*, so-called by the Ammonites (Deuteronomy 2:20-21); the *Emim* (Genesis 14:5; Deuteronomy 2:11), as the Moabites called them; and the

Rephaim (this seems to have been a general term that covered all these local names).

One translation calls them *titans* in 2 Samuel 5:18, 22. The term *Valley of the Rephaim* where King David fought the Philistines was translated *Valley of the Titans*, or *Valley of the Giants*. All of us will have to face the enemy in the Valley of the Giants.

The Bible's first detailed account concerning giants is the story of young David's encounter with Goliath, in 1 Samuel 17:17-54. David was sent by his father, Jesse, to check on the older brothers who were fighting at the front and to take them some food.

When David got there, he discovered the "mighty warriors" of Israel huddled in trenches—in total fear of the Philistine's champion, Goliath. He was about thirteen feet tall, and every day he openly challenged anyone in Israel's army to fight him.

Goliath was a big, dangerous man of war, but David was strong and courageous, and most importantly—he believed God was with him. David had used his weapons successfully in one-on-one battles with lions and bears. He had built his strength until he could fling a stone hard enough and with enough accuracy to bring down the beasts that threatened his flock.

No one from the thousands of mighty men of Israel dared to step up and meet Goliath's challenge until David arrived. Even King Saul's offer of his daughter's hand in marriage and the waiving of taxation failed to produce a champion to take on the giant.

David went through several tests after he reached the battle front. Once there, he declared his plan to meet Goliath in battle. His older brothers laughed and accused him of coming to show off. Even the king said, "You can't fight this Philistine! You are only a boy."

Then Saul tried to give David the king's armor, which was much too heavy and big. David had to be willing to go into

combat with no apparent protection, not looking like a soldier at
all. David had never fought men, yet he was about to face a
champion of champions. He was still a teenager, because in Israel, a man could be put into the army only after he turned twenty. David did not go into that battle with a cocky attitude, but he
did know in whom he believed. He said, "I fought a lion and a
bear, and the living God delivered me from their paws. I know
He will also deliver me from this 'uncircumcised Philistine'
who has defied the armies of God" (1 Samuel 17:36-37).

God knows the hearts of His children, whether or not we
will fight to win and have the spirit of a winner. He knew David
had faith to fight.

Each Christian in the Church today has the responsibility to
fight, but the question is: Do each of us have the faith to fight?
Do we trust the living God to save us? Do we have the heart of
a winner? We automatically stepped into the spiritual boxing
ring when we were born again. Whether we fight or lay down
and get trampled on is our choice.

David said to Goliath, "You come at me with man's
weapons, but I am coming at you with the name of the Lord"
(1 Samuel 17:45, my paraphrase).

The Key To Defeating Giants

The key to winning battles with giants is the same for us as
it was for David: go forth in the name of the Lord. The five
smooth stones David picked up while crossing the brook symbolize the Word of God. We shoot the enemy with the Word. To
Jesus, however, we **are** the living stones that He sends forth
from the Holy Spirit to conquer the enemy. We do not become
smooth stones without the washing of the water of the Word,
without rubbing off the rough places through fellowship with
the brethren. Stones rub other stones as the water washes over
them and tumbles them downstream.

Notice that stones in a stream are all under the water. We do
not become smooth stones when we are half-in and half-out of
the stream. When we are in a local church, we are in the water,
and the current moves us around. If a person just sits at home,
reads the Bible and prays, he might get smooth on two sides,
but God wants him to be well-rounded. Other people help make
us smooth on all sides. We have to be where the Word of God
can move us around, test us and prepare us. Those little stones
David picked up had been there for years, just waiting for him
to use them. They washed down into the valley from up on the
mountainside, maybe during a heavy storm.

Once those stones landed in that stream, they were there for
a long time, just waiting. Some people are like that. They may
have been washed down by storms into the house of the Lord
and have been sitting there for years, while the Spirit of God
prepares them for the Master's use.

Why is it important that we be "smooth stones" like the
physical stones David used? If you are not a smooth stone when
you are shot forth, you will wobble this way and that, not hitting
the target with any real strength. So stay where God puts you
and let yourself be tested and smoothed off for His use.

David said six things to Goliath in 1 Samuel 17:45-47:

1- You come with man's weapons, but I come in the name
   of the Lord.

2 - **This** day, not tomorrow or next week—but right now—
   the Lord will deliver you into my hand.

3 - I will smite you.

4 - I will give your carcass to the fowls.

5 - All the earth will know there is a God in Israel.

6 - All this assembly will know there is a God in Israel.

We need to take these six things to heart and use them
against our giants. Once we learn how to fight and deal with the

enemy, God will be able to restore more truths to the Church.
Then the Body of Christ will be that much closer to Jesus being
able to return.

The Five Giants

The Church, God's spiritual nation, has three big jobs to do:
first, she is to prepare for the coming of her Bridegroom, Jesus
Christ. This involves purification, dedication and separation.
Her second task is to proclaim the good news of His death and
resurrection to the lost world while destroying every work of
the enemy. And thirdly, her job is to occupy this earth as
caretaker and spiritual salt until His triumphant return.

Just as ancient Israel crossed the Jordan and faced giants
before possessing the land, the Church faces giants to battle
both without (in the world) and within her own ranks.

Five giants tower over us in the land today. Our job, as
blood-washed "boxers of the Lamb," is to knock these proud
God-haters out of the ring and out of our way. We've got a land
to possess!

The first giant challenging the Church is *Ishbibenob*
(2 Samuel 21:16), which means "to come from the land of
Nob— emptiness; has no fruit; destruction; to lark about; to
destroy; to snatch; to take away; to destroy fruitfulness."

Jesus warned us in the Gospel of John 10:10, that the enemy
always comes to destroy our fruit. He comes to steal, kill and
destroy.

A man of God named Abishai fought this giant in Second
Samuel. Abishai means "good; a person that is generous; a person that is available; fruitfulness; father of gifts."

Fruitfulness will always defeat emptiness. If you have the
fruits of the Spirit in your life and if you are living for God, you
will kill the giant of barrenness. You will always produce, no
matter how barren the land might be. When someone who is
full of the fruit of the Spirit witnesses to someone who doesn't

know God and has no fruit in his life, sudden fruitfulness comes
as that person receives Jesus. That's the way it works—when
someone who knows God and is full of the Spirit, begins to talk
to those who are empty and lifeless, then something has to give!
Fruit is produced in that other life.

The second giant shows up in verse 18 of Second Samuel
21. *Saph* is the giant of separation and division. *Saph* literally
means "to snatch away; kidnap; to take away illegally; an exter-
minator; terminator; separator; to separate; to take away from
whatever is there; kidnapper-illegal taker away of something."

Sibbebchai was one of the soldiers with David. His name
means "to wrap together, to entwine; to incorporate; to bring
unity." Just as David's champion, Sibbebchai, slew the giant
Saph, so unity will always defeat separation. Always!

That's the whole thing—if the whole Church could ever
come together...my heart is filled with a longing to see the
Body of Christ united, because it is the one area in which we are
defeated over, and over, and over, and over again.

We produce fruits and do all the good works, but then we
come home and are separated one from another. We will never
be able to fulfill the will of God unless we are wrapped
together, entwined together, and joined together as one in unity
in Christ.

The Church faces a third giant named *Lahmi*, the "counterfeit." Mentioned in Second Samuel 21:19, *Lahmi* means "show
bread; show off; plastic; counterfeit." This fellow used a
weaver's beam as the handle of his spear—in other words, it
was a huge beam. He was a mighty, powerful person. *Lahmi*
was a counterfeit.

There are those who will bring the counterfeit, the plastic
into the Church. Unfortunately, we see a lot of the leaders using
counterfeit methods today...they try to say that everything is
great and wonderful, that there are no testings. They say that we

can have anything we want, it's all prosperity, it's all joy—but somehow they leave out the cross.

The Bible says we must die daily. You have to pick up your cross and follow Him, and count it all joy. Without a cross there is no crown. There's a lot of "show bread" on television today. I'm talking about preachers who are just running a big con game. It's a big hustle. Those people are trying to get your money. Without the bloody reality of the cross and the miracle of salvation in lost and dying hearts, it's all plastic and make-believe.

Praise God, He always has a match for the devil's tricks and tricksters! *Lahmi* the Counterfeit Giant met his match in El-hanan, whose name means "God is gracious; He (God) is all-sufficient."

You see, there is the make-believe, the show bread, the plastic, the counterfeit and the fraud, and then there is that which is gracious, genuine and all-sufficient. God is gracious, God is enough, God is sufficient. The sufficiency of God is all you need to defeat the counterfeit giants in your life, and those confronting your church. God is gracious.

The fourth giant in Second Samuel 21:20 was a monstrosity with *no name*. He had six fingers and six toes on each hand and each foot—he was deformed. This no-name monstrosity is an oddball tower of strength who dared to taunt and jeer at God and His people.

There are a lot of oddballs out there roaming the religious streets and the religious corridors doing monstrous deeds.

Although I will deal with specific giants *within the Church* in the next chapter, this particular monstrosity thrives within the Church as well as without. He's deadly in both places.

No wonder the world looks at the Church and wonders what's going on. There are a lot of things that threaten the genuine Church today. This monstrosity roams freely through our cities, our legislatures, our choir lofts and our homes.

There are a lot of people doing things in the name of God that are so irrational, so unethical, so ungodly and so unscriptural that the world is shocked by it. They can't understand what is going on in a church that claims to be raising up giant-killers.

This is far from the scriptural pattern God intends for His people and for His leaders. Unfortunately, these giants are people who are looked to, who stand tall in the eyes of many, and they have a lot of followers. These monstrosities are oddballs; they are deformed.

These kinds of giants get into all kinds of perversions; still people follow them. They tear the scriptures to shreds. They violate every principle of the commandments and statutes of God and the decency, honesty and humility of Scripture. And yet, people follow them because they dress like Hollywood stars, they talk like Hollywood stars, they shine forth with worldly brilliance; God's people are taken in by it.

It's strange, but even the world looks at it and says, "This can't be God." And the world is right. Well, there is a God in Heaven Who is well able to defeat any giant hatched in the evil heart of the devil!

The no-name monstrosity who dared to taunt Israel was promptly killed before the gate of Gath (one of the cities of the giants) by Jonathan ("God has given; power; grace; authority"). When you face a monstrosity that is so evil and so contemptuous toward you that you can't even name it, remember 1 John 4:4b, *Greater is He that is within you, than he that is in the world.*

The fifth giant is the worst one—he is *Goliath*, whose name literally means "to denude; to make naked; to strip; to expose; to bring shame to one." *Goliath* arrogantly exposed the people of God and the army of God; he brought fear and intimidation into their hearts in First Samuel 17.

How often are we afraid to come out and meet *Goliath*, the denuder, the one who brings shame, the one who mocks and strips God's people?

The Lord always has a champion in the wings. He'd prepared a young, tender-hearted song writer and sheep-tender named David just for *Goliath*. David means "beloved."

You will never win the victory unless you love God with all your heart, and you live in His love. When you love God, giants are nothing to you. Even the "Goliaths" have no power great enough to defeat you.

In Numbers 14:8-9, it says, *If the Lord delight in us, He will bring us into this land and give it to us. A land which floweth with milk and honey. Only rebel not ye against the Lord, neither fear ye the people of the land, for they are bread for us. Their defense has departed from them and the Lord is with us, fear them not.*

Are you facing giants today? Is a *Goliath* standing between you and the fulfillment of God's promise to you and your church? Fear them not! They are bread for us.

David, the shepherd boy from the country, looked at 13-foot tall *Goliath* from the great city of Gath, and said, "You are bread for us." Every one of the great men of God who fought giants years later under the command of David must have remembered David looking at the hulking form of *Goliath* and saying, "You are bread for me." They remembered seeing David *run* toward the denuder, the one who brought shame and belittled them. Every one of them remembered David's unforgettable words, "You come to me with a sword and a shield, but I come to you in the name of the Lord of Hosts."

I tell you, that's what it takes to defeat the giants. You've got to come in the name of the Lord of Hosts.

THESE FIVE GIANTS FACE US TODAY AND THEY HAVE NEW NAMES!

Goliath's seed is determined to destroy God's seed. Like the days of old, his offspring seeks to kill, steal and destroy. One modern *Goliath* of our day is the giant of *abortion* that hates any seed made in the image of God.

The first *Goliath* bragged to the people of God, "Send a man to me and I will fight with him." Today, Goliath's ancient master still wants to destroy the seed of humanity, only he is doing it with the high-tech tool of government-subsidized abortion.

Giant number two is the giant of *humanism*. He is against God. He resurrects the first sin and temptation from the Garden of Eden, and says man can ascend to the greatness of God as a god himself.

The third giant is *homosexuality*. He is against creation, that which is normal. Satan delights in perverting everything God has made. The more beautiful it is, the more delicate and fragile it is, the more he loves to pervert, twist and defile it. Homosexuality strikes at the first institution set up by God in the Garden—the holy institution of marriage and the home.

The fourth giant has been sent to strike at morality. This giant, the giant of *pornography*, uses powerful bait to lure his victims to their death. He preys on human appetites to steal their souls and strip them of their weapons.

The last giant threatens our safety. This giant of *fear* stalks the streets. He is a monstrosity determined to steal our security and peace. He is the giant called murder (Matthew 10:39; John 10:10).

Round 13

The Enemy Within

Five enemies from hell stalk the Church of Jesus Christ today. They don't threaten from outside our walls, they rise up secretly from within our own number. These enemies are far more dangerous to the Church and more successful in their mission to pull her down than all the outside giants and obstacles put together!

The first of the five enemies threatening the Church from within is perfectly pictured in Absalom, the favorite son of King David who ultimately conspired to usurp the throne of Israel from him.

The Absalom Spirit

Absalom was born to David before Saul's death, before David had been officially installed as king. It is strange to see that Absalom's mother was Maacha, the daughter of Talmai king of *Geshur*. David and his men literally destroyed the Geshurites in First Samuel 27:8! The Geshurites were one of the original inhabitants of the Promised Land who should have been destroyed by Israel long before. David actually married the daughter of his enemies and had a son by her! How many times do we weave our own web of destruction, or at least contribute to it?

Later, after his father's reign was near its peak, Absalom worked and schemed around the clock to steal the hearts of God's people by deception, flattery and force. He wanted the whole kingdom, the whole ministry, the whole throne!

Absalom was driven by personal ambition and gifted with good looks and a charismatic gift of persuasion. His personality was so powerful that he successfully turned the hearts of an entire nation away from his famous soldier-king father, David! Absalom stood in a prominent place just outside his father's court and cunningly persuaded the people to follow him. Like those driven by this same spirit today, Absalom wanted his father's kingdom, his house and his throne. He even took his father's wives, the most sacred and inviolate part of his father's life. He wanted to rule the whole household.

The foul spirit that drove Absalom led him down a five-fold path to destruction: starting with a foundation of unnatural *ambition*, this spirit led David's oldest son into the depths of *pride, rebellion, deception* and *perversion*. Absalom ended up taking all of his father's concubines in an ultimate act of rebellious, perverted incest—in public!

Absalom's end clearly reflected his deepest character flaws. He literally died while suspended helplessly from a large tree by his long hair. Absalom's hair was the most visible symbol of his intense personal pride in himself—in the end, it caught him and directly contributed to his miserable and humiliating death. In the Bible, the tree always speaks of two things—flesh and fruit.

Absalom's life yielded the fruits of rebellion and disloyalty. Samuel the prophet describes Absalom's arrogant conspiracy against his trusting father in Second Samuel 15:12-13. As one of the three eldest sons of David, Absalom was under his father's authority—both in the family and under his civil rule as King.

It is wise to remember that the "Absalom spirit" generally shows its ugly head in a son or a relative, or someone who is close to you. If you are a pastor, or have a leadership role in a local church, and you see that spirit at work in someone, don't be surprised if they come in like an Absalom and try to undermine your authority. Absalom secretly stole the hearts of the people away from David.

People who yield to this spirit try to build their own kingdom. They often try to divide the local church by leading and teaching the people things that are contrary to the vision and direction God has given to the head pastor. Believers who are being manipulated by the spirit of Absalom are given clear warning by God before He deals with them. But He will deal with them—He has to, because this foul spirit causes strife and disunity in His flock that may cause wounds lasting for years.

Satan uses the Absalom spirit as one of his main attacks on a ministry or family—he does everything he can to divide and destroy it.

The Absalom spirit follows a pattern of infiltration and usurpation. The first attack is the most difficult to repel, because it comes in the form of conspiracy, in secrecy. This spirit quietly prompts Christian leaders or would-be leaders to talk—in secret—about their dislikes, their opinions and their solutions. ("All of it is in the best interests of the church, of course.") This "innocent talk" evolves into genuine conspiracy as the evil spirit behind it continues to work under the surface where no one sees it at work.

This is how it has begun in countless churches and ministries across the globe: as men and women join a ministry, they begin to work in various areas of ministry and prove their loyalty and commitment. Very often, they tackle the menial jobs no one else wants to do, and for their faithfulness, they get promoted to levels of leadership. As these zealous new leaders are raised up, they become of special interest to the satanic hierarchy, and evil spirits begin to target them because they are "the cream of the crop."

The Absalom spirit always works best in the cream of the crop—not the underlings. Why? The same traits that make some believers leaders can also fuel personal pride and ambition, and the cream of the crop—when lured into sin or jealousy or pride—can become satan's most destructive weapon against the Body of Christ under this spirit.

When satan's forces see a believer's zeal, they scheme to plant seeds of discouragement and discontent in their minds toward the other leaders, especially those over them. Being leaders themselves, they immediately begin to sow seeds of strife in other members of the Body.

Satan's plan is devious and simple: get young leaders to sow discord and division, and they will not only divide the present ministry, but will later on reap the same fate in future pastorates they might go into. So satan's two-fold plan is not only to destroy the local church today, it is to destroy the leader in the future with God's unchanging principle: what you sow, you will reap.

Any ministry an "Absalom" raises up or leads later on will be torn with the same type of strife and division and seeds of discord that he himself sowed. This device or plan of satan is at work with varying degress of success in every church in the world. God grants wise shepherds and sheep the grace and wisdom to stop these schemes at the door. The sad fact is that new churches don't know about this Absalom spirit, and just when these churches begin to get healthy, the devil comes right in and sows this thing over and over. If you see a church that has a move of the Spirit and a great pastor, and yet it doesn't grow— if you see split after split—then you know the spirit of Absalom is at work.

Examine yourself to see if the Absalom spirit is working in your life. Don't be offended—this spirit never tries to influence an evil person. It never seeks out a person with a malicious intention to destroy the ministry. This devious spirit must operate by influencing someone who is zealous to follow God.

Why am I devoting an entire chapter to these techniques of the enemy? I am following the example provided by Paul in the Bible. Paul told the church at Corinth that he was "not ignorant of his (satan's) devices" (2 Corinthians 2:11). Sadly, most churches today are ignorant of satan's devices.

God has raised up a standard against the enemy: the Word of God is our armor of defense (Ephesians 6:11).

Remember: the higher you rise in ministry and authority in a church, the more the evil echelon of demons and spirits want to deceive you because of your increased influence.

The enemy knows: 1) You can influence more people if you are deceived; 2) if you can be deceived, it will limit or destroy your ability to damage his evil kingdom; 3) every seed of strife he can get you to sow now, you will reap in your own ministry one day.

The enemy isn't particularly brilliant, he didn't come up with this on his own—this truth is in God's Word. All the things that you do—good or evil—will surely come back to you with interest (Galatians 6:7). Even as a modern Absalom schemes to undermine his pastor, he is literally crafting his own destruction, because one day he is going to reap everything he sows.

Strife is one of satan's greatest tools (2 Timothy 2:24-26). Any Christian who dares to help instigate strife among God's sheep is in desperate trouble—he has given place to satan who can take him captive at his will.

The spirit of Absalom always tries to inspire a conspiracy by secretly sowing seeds of strife (2 Samuel 15:12). Absalom carefully built a contingent of people who agreed with his ideas and followed his leading. David and the other leaders of Israel didn't know about it until it was too late, because Absalom worked behind the scenes, under the protection of their love and trust.

The most devastating betrayal always comes from within the circle of family or friends. King David wrote a painful passage about his trial in Psalm 41:9, echoing a tragedy destined to happen to the Messiah Himself, "Yea, mine own familiar friend, in whom I trusted, which did eat of my bread, hath lifted up his heel against me."

When Samuel begins his narrative about King David in Second Samuel 1:5, David was at rest from his enemies. He was enjoying the prosperity of a kingdom that "had it all together." When things seem to be going right, don't let your guard down. The devil never sleeps.

The Word of the Lord came to Nathan for David in Second Samuel 7:4-17. Verses 12 and 13 summarize God's prophetic promise to David:

And when thy days be fulfilled, and thou shalt sleep with thy fathers, I will set up thy seed after thee, which shall proceed out of thy bowels, and I will establish his kingdom.

He shall build an house for My name, and I will stablish the throne of his kingdom for ever.

If David had kept his nose clean, Absalom would never have gotten the foothold to do what he did, because his actions were also foretold by God after David committed a terrible sin. David committed adultery with Bathsheba and then arranged the death of her husband, Uriah the Hittite, a faithful member of his army. Nathan once again came to deliver the word of the Lord to the King—but this time he brought cursing, not blessing. God said the sword would never leave David's family. The original promise to establish the "throne of David" forever was not laid aside, but a curse was added to it because of David's sin. God specifically prophesied through Samuel the shameful acts Absalom would perform in the years to come.

Now, therefore, the sword shall never depart from thine house, because thou hast despised Me, and hast taken the wife of Uriah, the Hittite, to be thy wife.

Thus saith the Lord, Behold, I will raise up evil against thee out of thine own house, and I will take thy wives before thine eyes, and give them unto thy neighbor, and he shall lie with thy wives in the sight of this sun.

For thou didst it secretly: but I will do this thing before all Israel, and before the sun.

2 Samuel 12:10-12

The fourteenth chapter of Second Samuel describes one of the saddest relationships in the Bible, and one of the most common situations in American homes as well. David loved and trusted Absalom—*he loved him more than he loved right behavior, or God's law.* David consistently failed to discipline his sons according to God's instructions. Absalom was already a scoundrel, he had already had his brother Amnon killed for raping his sister, Tamar. David's household was a mess—he was unequally yoked with unbelieving wives (notice, he had many more than one wife—that spells trouble right there), he didn't actively participate in the rearing of his children, and when his children sinned, he just folded his hands and did nothing.

Absalom was wrong to plot the death of his brother, but David invited disaster because he didn't bother to do anything about Amnon—Absalom arranged Amnon's death two years *after* his crime against Tamar. It is unbelievable that David knew about the rape and did nothing. He is one of the most famous "absentee dad's" in history—look what it cost him!

David reluctantly banished Absalom from Israel after Joab and others protested the injustice of letting him get away with murder—but because he loved him so much, he let him back in after Absalom had spent three years in Geshur with his grandfather, Talmai. The first thing Absalom did after he returned to Jerusalem was to build his own little army. He wanted chariots and horses to run before him. When the people came to the gate to see the king with a problem, Absalom told them there was no one there to hear them.

The modern version sounds like this: "Oh, you know you won't get any of those pastors to minister to you. I really love you guys. I'm just available. If you have something you need a little wisdom on, let me help you." The original Absalom was undermining the king's authority. Modern Absaloms undermine the spiritual authority of pastors and other leaders in the ministry.

Absalom said, "Moreover, if I were made judge in the land..." He was basically saying, "I have as much as he has." He was building loyalty for himself. He showed great concern and affection for every person who was coming to see the king, but through it all he had an ulterior motive—a secret ambition.

The enemy of the Church tries to plant people in every local church who will constantly try to build a loyal base of followers for themselves through sympathy, favors and other means while saying little things to undermine the local church leadership. They are very sincere, at least in the beginning. They give comforting words to people—it can be very confusing, because members of the Body are supposed to comfort one another, they're supposed to operate freely in the gifts of the Spirit. But what is the motive of their heart in all of these actions? Are they building God's Kingdom or their own?

Absalom stole the hearts of the men of Israel. He won their favor to himself. True servants "steal" nothing—and everything they do should point to Jesus Christ and support His divinely established government in the local church. True servants build loyalty to the leader. They never want favor for themselves. They are like David's mighty men of valor, who risked their lives by sneaking through an army of hostile troops just to get a cup of water for David. They shared one heart and one goal—to make David king, to make him the anointed leader. When any subleader begins to build allegiance to himself, you've got an Absalom working in your ministry, in your household or in your office.

Absalom lost the spirit of obedience and servanthood—if he ever had it. The fruits we see in God's Word show us only the symptoms of pride, rebellion and selfishness.

Few leaders start out to be selfish. Disloyalty usually develops over a period of time when certain attitudes are allowed to settle into the spirit of a person with responsibility. Disloyalty does not happen overnight. No one wakes up one morning and finds himself "suddenly" disloyal. Disloyalty is an attitude that develops through various stages before it fully manifests itself.

Absalom sowed one seed that led to his downfall more than any other: *ambition. "Oh, that I were made judge in the land, that every man...might come unto me and I would do him justice!"* (2 Samuel 15:4). That same deadly seed is waiting to manifest in churches today: "If I were the leader, I could do a much better job of ministering to the people. I know God wants me to take over some leadership here, and I can do it to alleviate some of the pressure on the pastor. As I take over, the pastor won't have so much on his shoulders." That sure sounds godly, but its roots and fruit are devilish.

God (not man) placed the pastor at the top of His (not our) organizational structure of the church, and He sees the whole picture. The leadership support team may have good ideas, and they are to bring these ideas to the pastor. But they should never forget that the pastor sees the overall plan for the church.

The Absalom spirit gains a foothold in the church when a pastor turns down one of these ideas, and a leader decides to believe it is a personal affront to him. They may even say, "My idea was from God—how dare that man toss aside a 'word' from the Lord."

From that little incident a seed takes root in their soul. They are hurt. They may begin to murmur. At this point, satan implants the Absalom seed. *"You should have been the pastor. You could do a better job."*

The problem is these leaders often make two major mistakes: 1) they forget that the Church belongs to God, and He personally looks after the sheep and corrects wayward shepherds. The Bible is one massive record of God doing just that, in both the Old and New Testaments. 2) These leaders are usually focused on their small arena of responsibility, while the pastor is looking at the whole picture—after all, God will hold them personally responsible for their decisions and actions. Many times a pastor is maneuvered into a no-win situation. No matter what he does, he's the bad guy. The Absalom spirit must be dealt with in our churches.

The Spirit of Miriam

Miriam, the sister of Moses, is often remembered because she wanted equal authority with her brother. It didn't matter that God had sovereignly anointed and appointed him—in spite of his faults and apparent lack of qualifications. Her actions against Moses perfectly illustrate the devices used by a particular evil spirit threatening the Church today, the spirit of Miriam.

Miriam was a very gifted, intelligent woman. She was alert in her youth (Exodus 2:7). She was a recognized prophetess, and she had musical talents—she played the tambourine, and led the women in majestic praise and worship to the Lord in Exodus 15:21. But something was wrong somewhere in her heart. Perhaps it was serving so long just one breath away from the total authority wielded by her brother.... In Numbers 12:1-2, Miriam and Aaron spoke out publically against Moses, God's chosen leader. Notice that Miriam's name is first (which is unusual). This indicates that she was the instigator of this rebellion. Miriam and Aaron misused their family relationship when they decided to extend their disapproval of Moses' marriage to an Ethiopian woman beyond the family circle to incite rebellion in the nation: *"And they said, Hath the Lord indeed spoken only by Moses? hath He not spoken also by us? And the Lord heard it."*

Those five small words at the end of verse 2 should strike fear in the heart of every man, woman or child who decides to rebel against God's order. It sure frightens me! I don't know about you, but I don't want to say something against God's children when I know that *He hears it*!

People who rise up with a Miriam spirit want equal position, equal authority. They want to be considered as the pastor or the leader—they just don't like "playing second fiddle." They want to have the authority of the leader.

A unique characteristic of people under the influence of the Miriam spirit is that they will always find fault with something in the flesh against the leader. In the original situation, Miriam and Aaron (the sister and brother of Moses) basically said, "You can't be the only one to hear from God because you married this black woman."

This was their only complaint against Moses. Have you noticed that their complaint had nothing to do with ministry, it had nothing to do with his decisions as a leader. It had to do with something of the flesh.

When people rise up to claim equal authority with an established leader in the Kingdom, they generally try to find what they consider to be a weakness in the leader's flesh. In this instance, they griped about Moses' choice for a wife. Their complaint obviously speaks of prejudice in the heart of Miriam and Aaron. They weren't happy being a part of the "inner circle" of leadership—they were already "Number Three and Number

Two" respectively—they wanted *equal authority*, which means equal position and equal everything. We have that in the Body of Christ today, and we have always had it.

There will always be people who do not want to submit to God's anointed leadership. They always try to find one reason or another why the current leader should not be the one to lead, and since God doesn't pick people because they're "qualified" in the flesh, it's very easy to find visible faults in God's leaders. They forget that God supernaturally qualifies His leaders with supernatural gifts and grace.

Perhaps the leader doesn't pray as much as somebody else, or maybe he doesn't spend enough hours in his study at church to suit them—they'll drag up whatever they can think up against the flesh. It could be that he doesn't have sufficient education, or he doesn't speak well. They will find a reason to try to usurp authority and become equal. People following the lead of the Miriam spirit generally do not want to take over, but they want to be equal. They want the same thing the devil said he wanted—to ascend to the throne of God. He wanted to be equal with God. It is a satanic spirit, and it is a spirit of rebellion. Because of Miriam's sin, God allowed leprosy to come upon her.

Now when that spirit arises and God sovereignly moves to stop it, it causes the whole church to stop its progress. The entire nation of Israel was forced to stop its journey through the wilderness toward the Promised Land while Miriam waited *outside of the camp* for her period of uncleanliness to be completed. In the same way, leaders who rebel like Miriam have to be "put out of the camp" for a period of restoration; they have to be separated while their attitudes and actions come back into line with God's Word and plan for the local church.

There are at least two main reasons for this type of correction. First, Miriam and Aaron were family. Moses loved Miriam, in fact it was his intercessory prayer that prompted

God to reduce her sentence of affliction as an outcast leper, from life to only a matter of days.

People who rise up as "Miriams" and are caught and dealt with, are still "family." If they repent, they are to be restored. Moses never stopped loving Miriam or Aaron.

Secondly, Miriam sowed some unwanted, dangerous weeds in the family garden. Every one of those weeds has to be rooted out. God does this by publicly disowning their words, their authority and their position as "equals." He publically affirmed His anointed leader so there would be no doubt who was in charge and who was not. God will often publically humiliate "Miriams"—without the help of "Moses."

Modern "Miriams" go around the local church saying, "I don't agree with the pastor," or "The pastor is not always right—I hear from God, too. In fact, I think I heard from God on this situation or this subject, but the pastor just won't listen!"

Obviously Aaron and Miriam had been talking, and they looked down on Moses because he was their younger brother. They wanted to be in the same position. Now, we have to be careful with family. Sometimes when we put our family members into the ministry, after a while (especially with brothers and sisters), they may begin to feel that they should be equal. It causes great problems, and it usually doesn't work.

Later on, Aaron got into more trouble by listening to the people and seeking popularity. This happens a lot in the Church, too. It doesn't always work for pastors and leaders to put their own children in a place of authority in the same work. It is better if their children go to another area of ministry, start another church with their blessing, or go to the mission field. I am not saying that it doesn't work, it does once in a while—especially when the children start "at the bottom" and earn the right to lead through servanthood apart from family relationship.

Very seldom can a brother, a sister, or a son take over a work and be as successful as the parent before them. Usually, when they do take it over, they want to prove that they are as good or better than their father or mother, and it can become a competitive thing. It often turns into a curse rather than a blessing.

The Miriam spirit is in the Church, and it wants equal position and equal authority with God's appointed, anointed leader.

The Spirit of Korah

Another spirit plagues the flock of God in this generation—a spirit that has earned God's undying hatred and wrath. Korah, whose name means *ice, or bold, or forward*, started an open rebellion against God's leadership.

Korah said that Moses had too much authority, and he and his partners wanted a share of it. The first spirit we talked about was a son, the second one was a sister, and the third one is an elder or a prince. Korah was a leader in the tribe of Levi, the priestly tribe. He was a prince with limited authority over a certain segment of Israel's population. In the sixteenth chapter of the Book of Numbers, we are told that Korah gathered 250 leaders or princes of Israel like himself and made a bid for more power or control over the nation.

Korah and his bunch said that Moses had too much authority. Then Korah misused and misappropriated the same argument used today to justify rebellion and challenges to leadership in the Church. He used the "all believers are priests" argument to promote his hidden agenda.

> *And they rose up before Moses, with certain of the children of Israel, two hundred and fifty princes of the assembly, famous in the congregation, men of renown:*

> *And they gathered themselves together against Moses and against Aaron, and said unto them, Ye take too much upon you, seeing all the congregation is holy, every one of them, and the Lord is among them: wherefore, then, lift ye up yourselves above the congregation of the Lord?*

And when Moses heard it, he fell upon his face.

Numbers 16:2-4

Korah wasn't looking for equal leadership; he wanted complete control over authority. And he wasn't wanting to spread the authority to everyone in the congregation—in spite of his high-sounding words.

I have found in my travels and years of ministry that would-be leaders who want equal authority are generally not called to the five-fold ministry, but they want to control the five-fold ministers. Once a group of people operating according to the spirit of Korah get the upper hand and begin to control the pastor or senior minister, one leader will emerge from among them. This person will try to be the voice of these elders who now have assumed a position that has not been given to them by scripture or by godly authority. This type of "ruling junta" always has an agenda. In most churches today, the pastors have to adhere to a board, a totally unscriptural description of a governing group. The Bible speaks of the governors as apostles, prophets, evangelists, pastors and teachers—not boards, not laymen, but those who are called to the five-fold ministry.

Many denominations today have set up these boards. Usually, one man is the voice. He is the one who will take care of the pastor, and he will make sure that the pastor will do what the board wants. He is the one who knows how to "twist the tail of the pastor."

Korah was such a person. A deacon or elder who is not satisfied with his or her position, who aspires to gain control over God's authority, is operating under the influence of the Korah spirit.

I have seen a lot of churches destroyed because of this spirit. For example, we set a pastor in a church we started and nurtured. Unfortunately, there was a "Korah group" in the church, and this particular pastor wasn't strong enough to handle them.

Pretty soon that group took over and took charge. They finally talked the pastor into separating from us. That pastor did not last, and in fact, that group hasn't been able to keep a pastor since. The leadership of that church transferred between those men one by one, and each time, after a while, the men decided they didn't want to be the pastor—they just wanted to control the pastor.

This is very important: the Korah spirit does not want the total responsibility of pastoring; it just wants to control and manipulate the pastor and get its own agenda. Korah wants equal leadership power without equal responsibility.

What happened to Korah? The Bible says 14,700 people died in the rebellion along with the 250 princes and their families. All those who join a rebellion like this end up dead. They die spiritually, and they never get over the fact of what they did. Once a leper, always a leper! Even if you are cleansed, the scars and disfigurement of leprosy will always stay with you. Simon the Leper was with Jesus, but the leprosy still remained as far as the destruction that the leprosy creates in the body. You never come out right, even if you repent—the scars always remain with you and others will remember it.

I have had several sons, Absaloms, in my own ministry—I trained them and birthed them as far as leading them to the Lord, but in the end they brought havoc in our church. These Absaloms will always reap what they sow. In the end they die along with those who follow them in rebellion. I am not talking about innocent ones, I'm talking about the people who openly join their rebellious cause and fight for them and go into battle for them—they end up dead.

I have had Miriam spirits in the church. They don't want to take over, they just want to tell you that they hear from God too. You are not the only spiritual leader. They want the people to acknowledge them also as the spiritual leaders of the church. This form of rebellion brings leprosy.

Then I have had the Korahs, who rose up and won influence with other leaders, even taking these leaders out of the church

—they are all still wandering out there in the wilderness. Again, this brings death. Korah started with just two men, and those two influenced their families, and their families influenced others. In the end, 250 princes of Israel and their families, and 14,700 people died. That is what always happens in the end.

The Spirit of Achan

A character by the name of Achan appears in Joshua 7:1. Achan literally means *troubler*, or *one who caused trouble*. Achan's sin is very common in the church today. He stole the accursed thing.

After Israel had defeated an enemy in battle, Achan saw a "Babylonish garment" that he coveted, along with bars of silver and gold that were consecrated to the treasury. He secretly took them and hid them in the ground under his tent. His sin caused God's blessing and protective covering to lift from Israel, and it needlessly cost the lives of 36 soldiers. God was so angry with Achan's willful and deceitful theft of forbidden goods that he publically revealed Achan's sin before the entire nation. Achan and his entire family were put to death to remove the curse from Israel.

The accursed thing destroys anyone who touches it. It is important to understand that even holy and good things can be accursed to us—if they have been set aside solely for God. To take them or to disregard their separated status is to openly disregard God. Anything that is consecrated to the sanctuary for sacred use is holy—including the tithe. Achan stole from that which was set aside and it became a curse to him and his family, and to his nation.

I have been amazed and astonished to learn that there are many people who do not fear God. I came from the world of sin. I have seen and done some atrocious things. I stole other peoples' property, I robbed people at gunpoint, I burglarized...I committed all kinds of crime when I was in the world. However, when I came to the Lord, I had a great fear about touching the things that belong to God and taking unlawfully what was not mine.

I am astounded at the number of people who do not fear God today! We have caught people in our church stealing out of the offering plates in the counting room—they were taking twenty dollar bills from the plates and rolling them in their palms to put in their pockets. These were people in the House of God—some were even deacons who had been faithful in many areas in God's House—yet they weren't afraid to steal offering and tithe money from God! It astounds me that anyone would have the audacity and the fearlessness of God to do such a thing. It boggles my mind! That is the spirit of Achan at work.

The worst offenders operating under the influence of the spirit of Achan are those who insist on continuing their charade of active Christian service or even leadership—while all the time, they continue to arrogantly steal from God.

You'll see them praising and worshiping God, dancing before the Lord and even prophesying before the congregation. Sometimes they are teaching scripture in Sunday School, heading up groups, or even serving as deacons and elders—these are the worst offenders in God's eyes because while they seem to lead God's flock, they are robbing God and His people because they don't tithe.

I may be stepping on some toes, but the truth must be said. The spirit of Achan is alive and well—indeed, it's actually prospering in the Church today! Listen: people who don't tithe have an anti-church, anti-Christ spirit. If it was left up to them, they would close down every local assembly.

These disciples of Achan are parasites in the Body of Christ because they sit under the ministry, take in all that the ministry has to offer and enjoy all the benefits of the sanctuary but put nothing back in.

Modern-day Achans sit on the pews of every church in the world, enjoying the Sunday School and Vacation Bible School departments, sending their children to the daycare and the nurseries, enjoying the evangelists and prophets that come through. They take for granted the heat and the lights of the building. Somehow, it never occurs to them how all of those things are paid for. They don't ever stop to wonder how missionaries are sent around the globe, or how the pastor and his staff buy shoes for their families. Despite all the knowledge, all the teaching, and all the prompting of the Holy Spirit, they still will not pay their part to maintain the facilities and ministry for the Lord. The Bible says that they are a cursed people and should have no part in the things of God—no part at all. God says they are cursed with a special curse, because like Achan, these people destroy the House of the Lord by robbing the very God who gives them life.

The Judas Spirit

Judas was the betrayer of the Lord Jesus Christ. His betrayal of the Messiah was prophesied about in the Old Testament. You may be shocked to know that there are Judas spirits in every church today.

What are the characteristics of a Judas spirit? This spirit speaks wicked words. King David prophesied under the anointing of God about the betrayer of God's Son in Psalm 109:1-20. Verse 2 says he speaks evil words that are deceitful and full of lies. Verse 3 says he speaks words of hatred without a cause. He despises the love of good men (verse 4), and he returns evil for good and hatred for love (verse 5). In verse 6, this betrayer is called the agent of satan. A Judas can pose as a prayerful and holy man (verse 7). Verse 16 says this betrayer is unmerciful and an oppressor of the poor and needy, the murderer of helpless and innocent men.

The Judas spirit constantly accuses others—after all, this spirit's father is the father of lies and the accuser of the brethren. The Judas spirit makes average people become assassins of character. They will talk about others and create stories about people. According to verses 17-19, betrayers won't hesitate to curse somebody.

I have met people like that. I have even met pastors who curse when the people don't do what they want. People under the influence of the Judas spirit lack appreciation of blessings (verse 17). Blessings don't mean anything to them. They reproach good men and have a lack of pity and kindness (verse 25). In verse 29, they are adversaries of good men. This Judas spirit is in every church. Satan wants to plant the Judas spirit in rebellious hearts in the House of God for the express purpose of *betraying and killing the pastor*.

There are enemies without and within, but, praise God, we are not ignorant of the enemy's devices, nor are our weapons of warfare weak or insufficient! This is the decade of restoration, God's appointed season of restitution for the Church. The match is almost over. I'm ready to hear the final bell and collect the winner's reward!

THE FINAL ROUNDS:
Restoration and Revival

Fear not, O land; be glad and rejoice: for the Lord will do great things...

Be glad then, ye children of Zion, and rejoice in the Lord, your God: for He hath given you the former rain moderately, and He will cause to come down for you the rain, the former rain and the latter rain in the first month.

And the floors shall be full of wheat, and the vats shall overflow with wine and oil.

And I will restore to you the years that the locust hath eaten, the cankerworm, and the caterpillar, and the palmer worm, My great army which I sent among you.

And ye shall eat in plenty, and be satisfied, and praise the name of the Lord, your God, who hath dealt wondrously with you: and My people shall never be ashamed.

Joel 2:21, 23-26

Round 14

The Restoration
of All Things

Restoration is the theme of the Bible. The underlying reason for God's plan of salvation is to restore things to His original plan in the Garden of Eden. Restoration also means the bringing back to life and operation of something that already existed.

The critics of the Restoration Movement today imply that the things being taught are "new" and, therefore, suspect. However, the opposite is true; the things being restored were originally given to the early Church, but were lost or neglected during the Dark Ages. The same principles had been given in different form to the Israelites and then lost by being turned into dead man-made traditions, the "letter of the law" without the life of the Spirit.

In Ezekiel 37, the Lord spoke to the prophet about dry bones coming to life. Peter told the Jews in Jerusalem shortly after the Day of Pentecost that they should repent and be converted so that the times of refreshing could come (Acts 3:19). Refreshing resurrects dry bones, but sin and dead traditions make dry bones. The timetable for this supernatural restitution of all things is known only to God. He is under no obligation to conform to any charts or computations of man.

Satan the thief, the destroyer, the adversary of God's Kingdom, thought he had given the Church (and the Lord's plan for it) a knockout punch toward the end of the first century— even though he knew he had failed to defeat the Lord. But God is the Champion Boxer—He had already won the victory. It was simply a matter of time.

The enemy somehow hoped that he had won, because he had successfully defeated so many individual Christians over hundreds of years by stealing the revelation of God that had been given through Jesus and the early disciples.

The Church was in total darkness for over a thousand years, yet God sovereignly preserved a remnant of true believers who managed to co-exist with the established Church. The apostolic ministry and the gifts of the Spirit no longer operated in the Church, and the Great Commission (Jesus' instructions to all believers) was superceded by man's authority over church function and worship activity. The priesthood of all believers was no longer acknowledged, and the Body lost and forfeited its ability and commission to minister. This was then reserved for a select priesthood of "professionals."

Eventually, the Church became the state, governing directly or indirectly through religious pressure. It even lost (or purposely discarded) the knowledge of man's need for a personal salvation experience with God. From that dark time to our day, most people were taught that if a person was physically born into a "Christian" family, he was called a Christian. We now call those years "the Dark Ages."

The Spirit of God no longer guided the lives of Christians into truth (John 16:13). When we walk away from truth, we have to find something to fill the gap, to take its place. So the Church got caught up in traditions. The same thing had happened to the Pharisees of Jesus' day (Mark 7:6-9). It is one of the devil's favorite tricks: to get man to exchange truth for tradition (Romans 1:23-25).

The Church compromised Scripture to accommodate secular beliefs, catering to the flesh. Today, almost five hundred years after God supernaturally restored His truth to the common man, we still lay aside the commandments of God for our traditions. Many churches have instituted programs and activities in place of obedience to the Scripture.

They have set up a form of godliness, dressed up with all kinds of rites and decorations. It is human nature to try to reduce everything to a common denominator, to reduce God to a point that we can "manage" Him, understand Him, and keep our "humanness."

It is that "ite," *fear*. We are afraid to walk by the Spirit and not by sight (2 Corinthians 5:7). We want to cut everything down to human size, so we can "stay on top of things." Isaiah the prophet described the state which tradition brings:

Hear, ye deaf; and look, ye blind, that ye may see.

Who is blind, but My servant? Or deaf, as My messenger that I sent? Who is blind as he that is perfect, and blind as the Lord's servant?

Seeing many things, but thou observest not; opening the ears, but he heareth not.

The Lord is well pleased for His righteousness' sake; He will magnify the law, and make it honorable.

Isaiah 42:18-21

In spite of all of those who see or don't see, the Lord is going to magnify His Word, His law and His principles. Isaiah goes on to describe the people caught in tradition and doctrines of men:

But this is a people robbed and spoiled; they are all of them snared in holes, and they are hid in prison houses: they are for a prey, and none delivereth; for a spoil, and none saith, Restore.

*Who among you will give ear to this? Who will hearken
and hear for the time to come?*

                                        Isaiah 42:22-23

God is faithful, and He promises to restore the people of
God. Acts 3:21 says the heavens must receive Jesus until the
times of restoration. Restoration of what? The remainder of that
verse written by Luke is:

*...until the times of restitution of all things, which God
hath spoken by the mouth of all His holy prophets since
the world began.*

In the Greek, *restitution* means "to set something back again
into its original order." God has promised to restore the Church
to His original intent for Her: perfection, maturity, being con-
formed to His image. The word also means "to be completed, to
be finished," or "to bring about to its fruition in prosperity."

Martin Luther, hungering for something more than mere
rules, regulations and fear, began to study the Bible for himself
and "rediscovered" the doctrine of justification by faith.
Through the grace of God, he dared to challenge the religious
establishment of his day, and his stand opened the way once
again for man to know about and personally experience salvation through Jesus Christ.

Since 1500, God has continued to restore the things the
Church has lost. One truth He is restoring today is spiritual warfare, the knowledge that we have an enemy and are enrolled in
an army.

Several things have to happen for restoration to occur. There
has to come a wave of genuine repentance and cleansing. Holiness is required for man to really see and hear spiritual things,
and holiness only surfaces where there is a deep hunger for God
and His righteousness. As long as the Church is satisfied with
past moves of God and with present things of the world, the
spiritual climate is not ripe for restoration. Fresh revelations of
the truths of God cannot take root, develop and mature in
apathetic hearts and congregations. (Even with the right

climate, there will always be those religious people who fight
dogmatically against restored truth.)

Three Main Areas of Restoration

God is quickly restoring truth and knowledge to our generation in three main areas:

1. *The credibility and absolute truth of His Word.*

2. *The Renewal of fellowship with Him* as a result of applying His principles to our lives, bringing about a restoration of the existence and supernatural operation of His
   people, the Body of Christ.

3. *The completion of God's plan for the ages,* hinging on
   the Church's rediscovery and Spirit-led application of
   these biblical truths.

Everything that has been restored over the past five hundred
years is unmistakably rooted in the Word of God. He wants us
to get back to the simplicity of believing His Word. The truth
that makes us free is found in the Bible (John 8:32).

To have the truth is to be secure and confident. Then we will
not be argumentative, not determined to prove how steeped in
error the other guy is. Truth frees us from having to prove anything. Tradition forces us to constantly "prove our rightness" to
protect or hold on to our position; it divides the brethren. The
kind of spiritual renewal God wants comes from applying the
Word of God to every area of our lives. Tradition is religious, it
busies itself making us acceptable to the world. Tradition is
death—spiritual fellowship with God and one another is life.

The restoration of the Body of Christ begins with unity.
Without knowing that we are all "parts" of equal value to God,
we cannot come into unity. Until we realize that no one group,
local church, denomination or organization has an exclusive
claim to the whole truth, we will not work together.

Paul wrote, *The Body is not one member, but many.* In his
detailed teaching in First Corinthians 12, he makes it clear that

every part of the Body of Jesus is of equal value to God. We must allow God to restore this truth to us, or be doomed to honor our traditions instead of Jesus. We will continue to fight among ourselves, and find ourselves fighting against God at times—while we continue to believe we are "doing Him a favor" (Philippians 3:6).

Why is God bringing renewal to His Church? Look at the state of the Church today, then remember that according to Ephesians 5:25-26, God's Son will return one day for His Bride, His Church "without spot or wrinkle." The renewal of the Church is mandatory before our Lord returns!

The completion of God's plan for the ages will bring Jesus back as King of kings and Lord of lords, the eternal sacrificial Lamb and Priest of God. It will once again place man in dominion over the planet to fulfill whatever God's original purpose was for man and the earth.

Jeremiah the prophet gave us several signs of restoration to look for.

> *The voice of joy, and the voice of gladness; the voice of the Bridegroom, and the voice of the Bride; the voice of them who shall say, Praise the Lord of hosts; for the Lord is good; for His mercy endureth forever; and of those who shall bring the sacrifice of praise into the house of the Lord. For I will cause to return the captivity of the land, as at the first, saith the Lord.*

> Jeremiah 33:11

The restoration of true praise and worship in the Church is the fulfillment of Jeremiah's vision of "the voice of joy and of gladness." God wants to restore worship to the place where we can once again "worship Him in spirit and in truth" (John 4:23-24).

The "voice of the Bridegroom" is the restoration of the reality of Jesus through the Church. Those churches that are moving toward unity, that love one another, and that show love toward the unsaved, are the voice of Jesus in the land today.

The Church's place in society began to be restored in the United States and other countries during the late 1970's and 1980's. That brought much persecution and God began to earnestly cleanse His Temple, lest we bring even more reproach on His name, as the Church of the Middle Ages did.

The "voice of the Bridegroom" will be heard more and more through the "voice of the Bride," if we come together so that God can bring a sweeping revival. The Church will receive clearer direction and guidance from the Holy Spirit because our eyes will see and our ears hear the Word of the Lord.

The fourth thing that precedes God's removing us and the earth from captivity forever is "the voice of those who praise the Lord being heard in the land." As revival breaks out, believers will publically raise their voices in praise to the Lord.

The final thing to be restored to the Church is supernatural and worldwide revival and evangelism: the Church will be God's instrument to preach the gospel of the Kingdom "to the ends of the earth" (Matthew 24:14).

After that, according to the words of Jesus while he was on the earth, "*the end will come. After that will come the last trumpet*" (1 Corinthians 15:22; 1 Thessalonians 4:16). (There is nothing in these passages about us being "raptured out" before the Kingdom is preached to all the world.)

Kingdom truth is coming forth in our day. Many ask, "What is Kingdom truth?" Jesus' explanation and description of the Kingdom of God to the Jews of His day is scattered throughout the Gospels. A diligent study of the Bible reveals a detailed picture of what Jesus meant by "the Kingdom."

The Apostle Paul also wrote much about the Kingdom, and he summed it up for believers of all time with these words:

For the kingdom of God is not meat and drink; but righteousness, and peace, and joy in the Holy Ghost.

For he that in these things serveth Christ is acceptable to God, and approved of men.

*Let us, therefore, follow after the things which make for
peace, and things with which one may edify another.*

Romans 14:17-19

Unity, love and preferring one another: these are characteristics of Kingdom living. For those who might see Kingdom
life as humiliating and "wimpy," the Holy Spirit also inspired
Paul to write:

For the kingdom of God is not in word, but in power.

*What will ye? Shall I come unto you with a rod, or in
love, and in the spirit of meekness?*

1 Corinthians 4:20-21

Paul was warning the rebellious and the apathetic believers
of his day, "The Kingdom of God means submission to
authority, obedience to the Holy Spirit and the Word of God. If
we straighten up our attitudes and our deeds, then we can ap-
proach each other in love and meekness. Paul said, "If you do
not straighten up, I will come with the "rod" of the Word and
chastise you. The choice is yours."

Kingdom living is not just having our needs met, or ac-
quiring the desires of our heart through faith. God holds us
accountable for what He has given to us. We must submit to
God, exactly as soldiers are expected and made to operate
under authority in an army. Believers have no right to
criticize, judge or come against their fellow soldiers in any
way. It is a Kingdom truth that blessings demand responsibility
and accountability.

The "Restoration Movement" has been misunderstood and
fought by those still in the traditions of past movements. On the
other hand, some Christians have taken the truths of restoration
to the extreme.

Two quick ways to get "knocked out of the ring" by the
enemy are to; 1) ignore the things God restored to us to more effectively "box" the enemy, and 2) to misuse or abuse them.

We need to compare the teachings we hear with God's unchanging Word. We need to test every interpretation of His Word with the Holy Spirit's witness to our spirit—not merely by our intellect.

The mind will bring up as "truth" all the things we have believed or been taught in the past. If we are receiving restored truth, the first thing we have to fight is all the traditions we have formerly believed. We have to "cast down imaginations" and "every high thing that exalts itself against God" (2 Corinthians 10:3-6). Those things often include religious thinking and traditions as well as demonic or secular philosophies and beliefs.

The Restoration Movement

There are many individuals and churches in this day who are determined to see all the things lost by the Body of Christ restored in this generation. They believe God fully intended for His truths and gifts to be cherished and utilized by the Church until His return. These truths include the biblical doctrines of justification by faith, water baptism, laying on of hands in healing, the operation of the gifts of the Spirit, and now, in the 1990's, the restoration of each of the five ministries given to the Church by Jesus Christ (see Ephesians 4:8-12).

Were you taught that "speaking in tongues" is not for today?

Did you believe that God puts sickness and disease on people to teach them something?

The Holy Spirit is quickly wiping out these traditions and doctrines of men, yet many Christians still hang on to their traditions, just as in Jesus' day.

Kingdom truths don't appeal to the flesh, so they have always been revealed to a remnant, then slowly grown to become accepted by the majority. That point is where the danger comes in again: the enemy comes back for another round and does his best to turn that restored truth into tradition.

Kingdom living, then, means never sitting down, but always moving forward. The disciples of Jesus Christ must always contend or "box" with the enemy for the reality of the faith of the Father, Son and Holy Spirit. Kingdom living includes the restoration of Kingdom discipline as God intended it and as the apostles set forth for the Church in the New Testament. The same principles applied to Israel in the Old Testament. With the Holy Spirit living inside us, we can keep those principles and live at a higher spiritual level than they could.

Ever since our Lord's victory at Calvary, God's law has been written on our hearts (consciences) instead of on stone tablets, but His law has never changed. Jesus came to make it complete, to fulfill the heart of the law within us perfectly (Matthew 5:17; Ephesians 4:12-16). That also means we have a greater accountability than the Israelites.

Jesus prophesied to the cities of Chorazin, Bethsaida and Capernaum that they would receive a worse punishment than the cities of Tyre and Sidon, and even the legendary "sin city" of Sodom, because while these cities sinned before God, they never had the opportunity to hear and see the marvelous ministry and receive the gospel from Jesus Christ in person as did the three cities He visited so often.

He said it would be better for those ungodly cities in the day of judgment than for the cities of His own day (Matthew 11:21-24).

The same thing faces us as servants of God under the covenant of grace today: we have greater opportunity and greater accountability than any generation before us.

Those in the Restoration Movement want to restore church government to its former, God-ordained position. Many local church governments in our day do not follow the patterns set forth in Scripture.

A key truth that is vital to the restoration of the Church is the purpose, operation and authority of the *five ministries* Jesus sovereignly set in the Body (Ephesians 4:11). The Body of

Christ must be restored, and the five-fold ministries as well. But sadly, many churches will not accept prophets or apostles for today. We must teach "modern" believers to be committed to their local church so they can reach maturity and fully develop their gifts and callings in Christ.

The ministers of God must present a solid, unbroken message to believers who are inclined to wander without commitment: If you are "not being fed" somewhere, then seek God earnestly to find the place where He wants you, but do not use that as an excuse to be a "spiritual gypsy." God wants to plant you where you can bloom (1 Corinthians 12:18; Psalm 68:6).

Commitment is one of the foundational themes of the Restoration Movement, and is a biblical doctrine. Along with this commitment to a local church comes the responsibility of the pastor and leaders to bring about total involvement of the believers. Believers do not grow by sitting on pews with their mouths open to be fed, like little birds. If that's all they need, then Jesus went to a lot of wasted effort working with His ragged bunch of followers for three years. They should have just camped out at the nearest synogogue or established their own little Bible school to "receive the Word."

Jesus set the example. He knew that disciples learn by seeing and doing. Like newborn birds in a nest, the day comes when they must learn to fly, to look for their own food in the Word, and to do whatever the leadership asks them to for the good of the Church.

God has also placed a burning desire in His people to restore the biblical practice of the "laying on of hands" to set people into the ministry. God sent his prophets and priests to anoint Israel's kings and priests in the Old Testament, and He led the apostles in the first century to do the same for deacons, elders and apostles under the New Covenant. The scriptural principle is strong: the calling of God is to be confirmed by the anointing

and laying on of hands by those already set in places of
authority and leadership by God.

The final focus of the Restoration Movement is the operation of the spiritual gifts in all of their fullness in the local
church as described in detail in Roman 12:4-8 and First Corinthians 12:1-11.

The basic "text" of the Restoration Movement is Romans
12:1-5:

> *I beseech you therefore, brethren, by the mercies of God,
> that ye present your bodies a living sacrifice, holy, ac-
> ceptable unto God, which is your reasonable sacrifice.*

> *And be not conformed to this world, but be ye trans-
> formed by the renewing of your mind, that ye may prove
> what is that good, and acceptable, and perfect, will of
> God.*

> *For I say, through the grace given unto me, to every man
> that is among you, not to think of himself more highly
> than he ought to think, but to think soberly, according as
> God hath dealt to every man the measure of faith.*

> *For as we have many members in one body, and all
> members have not the same office,*

> *So we, being many, are one body in Christ, and every
> one members one of another.*

Paul spends the rest of the chapter explaining how this
works in practical terms. Everyone should respect the gifts and
callings of others, everyone should love one another with true
brotherly love and prefer one another. Believers under the law
of grace should be diligent and faithful about the Lord's business, rejoicing in hope and being patient in tribulation, being
quick to pray and equally quick to give to saints in need.

He even starts "meddling" (hitting those touchy, sensitive
areas), by saying we should bless those who persecute us, and

refuse to return evil for evil; we should be honest and live in peace with everyone as much as is possible.

Finally, Paul manages to offend "God's cops" everywhere—you know them, they're the ones with a heavenly mandate to try, convict and sentence believers who don't meet their standards—by saying that followers of Jesus must leave vengeance to God (no retaliation), and overcome evil with good.

Chapter 13 of the Book of Romans is actually a continuation of the same teaching and begins with the words: "Let every soul be subject unto the *higher powers...*" That, too, is Kingdom living.

Believers and Government

The Apostle Paul told believers to be subject (submissive to, or coming under the authority of) to higher powers *for there is no power but of God* (Romans 13:1-2). The principle of delegated civil and spiritual authority was ordained of God. Anyone that resists the ordinances (laws) of God, or the powers ordained by God, will be in danger of damnation. God ordained order, structure and government for the purpose of fulfilling His plans. Without godly order, God's divine purpose in our lives, our family, our church, and our country cannot be fulfilled. "Doing your own thing" is really a spirit of antichrist; that is why the enemy is bringing up a "punch" in the nineties that seems stronger than ever against the Church and the nation: a spirit of lawlessness.

Those who were assigned to uphold the law in this nation are the ones who (since World War II particularly) have done the most to subvert it. Unfortunately for the United States, various members of the legal profession have brought our laws to total chaos in regard to the moral standards of God. They have so twisted and disfigured the ordinances of the land and the provisions of the Constitution "in the name of civil liberties" that we cannot believe in justice anymore. Legal minds *permeated with high things that exalt themselves against God* have perverted the law itself. The very individuals who are destroying the law are the same people who are appointed to uphold it. Many of them studied law with the purpose of finding out how to break it "legally."

How does the Body of Christ fit into all of this mess? What should individual Christians do to restore the true law of righteousness to their land and communities?

First, we must always remember that *all authority* begins with God. He set boundaries for the earth itself, for the seas, for the elements, and for man as well (Job 14:5; 26:10).

Then God established three human institutions *to uphold His authority* and *to train people to live orderly*, according to His principles.

1. *The Family*—We are supposed to learn God's will in the context of our family environment. Someone said that the family is a "mini-church," a reflection of God's eternal purposes in Heaven and on earth. This is why the enemy brings his heaviest blows against the family through homosexuality, adultery and divorce, crime and addictions among teenagers, demonic music and entertainment films, and the most deadly of all: abortion. Ministers above all must never be too busy "about the Lord's work" to win their own children to Him.

2. *Civil Government*—God established government to bring order to society. In Romans 13:3-4, Paul said governments were responsible for punishing the wicked, and honoring, protecting and supporting the good. The devil has managed to land another strong knockout punch at this nation to subvert civil government. We cannot count on the wicked being punished and the good protected in our communities anymore. We must pray and wage warfare on behalf of our civil governments before it is too late.

3. *The Church*—The Body of Christ was put in place to be God's spokesman on earth, the Bride who is the "*voice* of the Bridegroom." We are to be the equippers of the family and the

conscience of the nation, the ambassadors of the Creator. Instead, we have become the compromiser, almost like the boxer who throws the fight to avoid "slugging it out" any longer.

The Church is experiencing heavy oppression and persecution around the world because it has compromised the principles of God for convenience for hundreds of years.

In Mexico, priests cannot wear their robes outside of the church now. In many Latin American and even European countries, churches are not permitted to have television programs.

Take heart, believer. This state of affairs will not last. I know that because the Word says so. Paul wrote that Jesus is coming back for "a glorious Church" in Ephesians 5:27.

When the Church ignites the torch of righteousness and holiness the way it's supposed to, the brightness of the glory of God will be seen throughout the world.

Then will come the great revival to take the gospel of the Kingdom to the ends of the earth. The bell will ring, and we will enter into the fifteenth and final round of our fight against the ancient enemy of God.

Round 15

The Five R's to Revival

It's been quite a fight. God, our manager, is still in our corner. The bell has sounded.

There are a number of things that Christians must do in order to fight the fifteenth and final round as God's earthly representatives in our battle with the devil.

When we enlisted, we were thrust into "the boxing ring." When we were reborn in Christ, we entered a fight with an enemy who is not going to give up until he is destroyed!

We learned how to fight and *win* our day-to-day battles by accepting God's restoration of all of the truths given to God's people from the beginning. We must be so committed to total victory through Christ that we never give up—even to the point of physical death (Philippians 1:20). (This last statement shouldn't sound so strange—countless believers choose to follow Christ every day in the face of death on every continent in the world—including North America). Bishop Jessy Winley said once to me before his death, "Brother John, when Christians loose the fear of death, man, then they are going to become real trouble for satan."

In addition to our personal commitment to Christ Jesus, we must know "the five R's" that lead to revival in a local church, a community and a nation.

1. *Revelation knowledge* of God's will and His purpose, and a clear understanding of where we are in relation to that purpose.

2. *Repentance*, turning away from sin and turning totally to God.

3. *Reconciliation.*

4. *Restoration*, which follows repentance and reconciliation.

5. *Rejoicing*, the capstone or end product of true revival.

The story of the prodigal son is a classic illustration of these five steps (Luke 15:11-32).

This rich boy had to get absolutely down and out with nowhere to go before he would receive the *revelation* that he was in a pig pen—only then did he realize that his father's house was where he belonged. He humbled himself, genuinely *repented* and set out to return.

Once he reached his father, there was *reconciliation.* The son was reconciled to the father. The father had not gone anywhere. He had not left the son; it was the other way around.

Once he received the *revelation* of his low state, *repented*, and was *reconciled* to his father—the son was *restored* to a position better than his former place. Then there came great *rejoicing* for everyone in the household (except the elder brother)! The "religious" older brother's self-righteousness almost caused him to miss the party.

Each time the "five-R's" occurred in the Church during the past five hundred years, great revivals swept across the land.

If we do not win the victory in our generation, the next generation will have to come into the ring and continue the battle.

Revelation Knowledge

Daniel, one of the most amazing and profound prophets in scripture, says in Daniel 2:22 that God reveals the deep and secret things. Another witness says in Amos 3:7 that God will do nothing without first revealing it to His prophets.

God uncovers the dark or hidden things because He is light. Jesus said in Matthew 10:26 that nothing is covered or hidden from public view that shall not be revealed. God is going to open the book on everything.

Revelation knowledge is vast, ranging from the Holy Spirit exposing the hidden dark places of our heart to His revelation to God's prophets today about what He is going to do next in individuals, in the Church and in the earth.

God did not destroy Sodom and Gomorrah without letting Abraham know so that he could intercede. He did not destroy Nineveh without letting Jonah know so that the people there could repent.

God is revealing to the Church its condition (Philippians 3:15). He is measuring the nations. The Soviet Union has discovered that its system of government is bankrupt and was never valid. God exposes the condition of darkness in individuals, nations or the Church so that repentance can come.

Repentance

When King Solomon completed the first temple ever built for God, he blessed God and offered prayer for his nation. In Second Chronicles 7:14, the Lord appeared to Solomon by night and spoke these unforgettable words: *If My people, which are called by My name, shall humble themselves, and pray, and seek My face, and turn from their wicked ways; then I will hear from Heaven, and will forgive their sin, and will heal their land.* God didn't tell Solomon that the world or the heathen nations had to repent, He said *My people, which are called by My name.*

In ancient civilizations, people would tear their garments to show intense sorrow and repentance, but Joel 2:13 says God's people should rend their hearts and not their garments. True repentance comes from the heart, and is not mere remorse. There is a difference between being sorry for your sin and being sorry you got caught. There is a difference between repenting for a sin and repenting because you have to deal with the consequences of that sin. There is a difference between seeing your own faults and seeing someone else's, just as there is a big difference between contending for the faith and striving for your own opinions. God wants us to repent for our own sins, to examine our own hearts. In Acts 3:19, we are urged to be converted that our sins may be blotted out.

The Bible says that all have sinned (Romans 3:10, 23). We can look as holy as we like and say every holy-sounding, "churchy" phrase we know. We could buy ourselves a pair of wings and flutter around like the birds pretending to be angels, but if our hearts were suddenly exposed by the Holy Spirit, each of us would fall to our knees crying, "Forgive me, Lord."

I'm not describing salvation, but sanctification, the work of the Holy Spirit to conform us to the image of Christ. I repent every day. If I say something I should not, or fail to say something I should have, I must repent. If I have an attitude in my heart against someone that is not love, I have to repent. When we do, say or think something against or contrary to the character or principles of God, we offend Him. We offend His righteousness, and we must repent. That is the on-going process of sanctification.

Reconciliation

Paul said that "the ministry of reconciliation" was given to the Church once God had reconciled us to Himself by Jesus Christ (2 Corinthians 5:18-19). Paul did not say God had to be reconciled to us—it was the other way around.

Through our earthly "father," Adam, our race walked away and came into enmity with God, yet our heavenly Father never stopped loving us or working to turn us back toward Himself once again. God knew the only way to do that was to allow His only begotten Son to sacrifice Himself. That's how much God loved us and wanted us to be reconciled to Him. After Jesus returned to the Father, we were to extend His ministry of reconciliation to the world. Praise Him!

Paul said in Romans 5:10 that while we were still enemies to God, we were reconciled to Him through the death of His Son. In the Old Testament, although Joseph's brothers had sinned against him, they were graciously reconciled through Joseph's personal sacrifice and his doing the right thing under persecution as a foreigner in Egypt. Joseph was a picture, a type of Jesus Christ, the Messiah and Savior.

Our personal assignment as members of the Church regarding the ministry of reconciliation is not an option; it is a call of God. Reconciliation does not mean schism. Anybody who is causing separations and divisions in the Body of Christ is literally working for anti-Christ.

Once you are reconciled, your former relationship can be restored to God, and that same relationship of love and grace should exist in all of your earthly relationships. Most of the time, restored relationships are better than the original.

Restoration

David was *restored* after he committed adultery, but he went through this same process: *revelation knowledge* from Nathan the prophet (2 Samuel 12:1-14), *repentance, reconciliation* to God, *restoration, rejoicing* and then revival.

David had a renewed awareness of how important His relationship with God was, and how blessed he had been. This is revealed in some of the Psalms written during and after his restoration (Psalms 61-69, and from Psalm 119 on).

Solomon was the result of this revival, a son of a reconciled union, a man blessed beyond any other Israelite king, and the Bible says the Lord loved him (1 Samuel 12:24).

Peter was restored after he publically denied Jesus three times—even though Jesus clearly taught that if any man denied Him before men, He would deny them before the Father (John 21:15-17, Matthew 10:33). The difference between the sentence and the pardon was true repentance and divine restoration by grace. Peter left the past behind and became one of the greatest apostles of all time in his work for the Kingdom.

The Jews were restored through this same five-fold process when Daniel received a *revelation* that it was the prophesied time to return to their homeland as he studied the sacred scrolls (Daniel 9:2). Daniel *repented* on behalf of the nation, which was *reconciled* to God, miraculously *restored* to the land with great *rejoicing*, and later experienced *revival* under Ezra.

Jerusalem itself was restored through the reconciliation ministry of Nehemiah, which involved the literal rebuilding of the walls. God always uses a man to point the way. He always gives the ministry of reconciliation to one of His children.

The Church must go through this same process, but when it is complete, we will see such rejoicing that the world cannot help but notice. The rejoicing will lead to revival. We sing that old song in many churches, "Oh, Lord, revive us again." But we do not want to pay the price to be revived: revelation knowledge of sin, repentance, reconciliation, restoration and rejoicing.

Rejoicing

When the father in Jesus' parable gave the "welcome home party" for the prodigal son, there was such rejoicing that you could hear it a long way from the house. The oldest son, who had been out in the fields, heard music and dancing as he drew closer to home.

If enough of us return to God and reach the stage of rejoicing, *our religious older brothers* will hear about it! Thank God for them! Thank God they remained faithful to the Father, although their motives may not always have been right. They stayed faithful while others ran off to spend the talents and abilities God had given them "in riotous living."

Those faithful older brothers get the first opportunity to hear the rejoicing and receive a revelation of their own sins. Then they can go through the same process to get to revival. (There are no shortcuts—for anybody!) After that, the world will hear the sounds of the party spread throughout the whole triumphant Church!

Then the fifteenth round with the enemy will be over, and he will be given the final knockout blow. God, the Champion Boxer, will have brought His children to their God-ordained position as all-time, blood-bought champions of the universe!

The Biggest Hindrance To Revival

I believe the greatest hindrance we have to reaching this ultimate victory is this: we do not have the total revelation that God is God!

This is God's planet, God's universe, and we are all His creations. Either we belong to Him, or we belong to the devil. Don't believe man's boasts or the media facade: no one in the entire world belongs to himself or herself.

We need to understand there is one God, one Church and one faith—not several faiths "all of equal value." We need to understand that there is one Head of the Church—Jesus Christ (Ephesians 5:24).

Jesus is the Head, and first in all things: He is the nourishment and the sustenance of the Body of Christ (Colossians 1:18; 2:19). No one gets to the Father except through Jesus (John 10:9).

The second thing we need is the realization of what God intended the "family" to mean. The Church is a family, and each member of this family has a place and a part to play. If we had the warm, caring family relationships that God intended, it would be easier to see the Church as a great, unstoppable family, as eternal brothers and sisters.

The third revelation we need is to understand that the body has many members. Each member of the Body of Christ is literally connected to the other by the blood ties of our covenant relationship with God through Jesus.

We are a spiritual body, with each member having different functions, and each function is important. We are dependent on one another in ways we never see. Many people's lives are shortened, Scripture says, because they do not properly discern the Body of Christ when they take Communion (1 Corinthians 11:29).

Every gift and ministry in the Church should be working together to reveal Christ in themselves and to the world. For each of us to fulfill our particular calling, we must recognize that we are members one of another and joint-heirs (Mark 9:15), equal heirs, to Jesus. We must have peace with one another and seek one another's well-being (Hebrews 10:24-25). We must always try to strengthen, edify, encourage and uplift one another (Romans 14:19).

When we finally receive the revelation that God is the Supreme and Sovereign Owner of the universe and of us, and that we do not belong to ourselves because we have been bought with a price (1 Corinthians 7:23), three things will follow: we will see and recognize the supernatural Church for what it is (the revelation of the Body), we will understand, appreciate and participate in its functioning and purpose; and we will begin to live like a true family.

My prayer is that you and your family will come into that saving knowledge and become good soldiers, good "boxers" for the Lord. I yearn for and dream of the day when we will come together as a spiritual Family of the Body of Christ with the total recognition of God's sovereignty. He is Lord, and we are servants. He is our Father, and we are His children (thanks to Jesus Christ). The outcome of the battle is secured. Our Heavenly Champion is Lord of all! My prayer for you is the same prayer that Paul wrote to the Christians at Ephesus:

For this cause I bow my knees unto the Father of our Lord Jesus Christ,

Of Whom the whole family in Heaven and earth is named,

That He would grant you, according to the riches of His glory, to be strengthened with might by His Spirit in the inner man;

That Christ may dwell in your hearts by faith; that ye, being rooted and grounded in love,

May be able to comprehend, with all saints, what is the breadth, and length, and depth, and height,

And to know the love of Christ, which passeth knowledge, that ye might be filled with all the fulness of God.

Ephesians 3:14-19

To all of you who believe and receive this message, join with us at Rock Church and other churches who are working toward unity in the Body.

Join us as we pray for God to bring His people to the place where we all are ready for the fifteenth and final round in the battle against satan. Then, God the Boxer will receive the Kingdom, the power and the glory for ever and ever and ever and ever.

Amen.

Epilogue

This one thing I do know, that until the Body of Christ becomes the catalyst for the answer to John 17:21-22, Jesus Christ will not return.

The prayer of our Lord and Savior, which is perhaps the most profound request in Scripture, that the Church would be "One"—must be answered by our coming together in one spirit, one mind, one faith in the togetherness of His love.

Then, shall we see Him face to face!

Other books by John and Anne Gimenez

Upon This Rock	John and Anne Gimenez
The Gathering	John Gimenez
Be Ye Possessed (Booklet)	John Gimenez
Healing the Fracture	John Gimenez
Whose Kingdom Is It Anyway?	Anne Gimenez
The Emerging Christian Woman	Anne Gimenez
Marking Your Children for God	Anne Gimenez

To order additional copies of *God the Boxer*
and other publications by John and Anne Gimenez,
please call or write:

Gimenez Evangelistic Association
P.O. Box 61777
Virginia Beach, VA 23466
(804) 495-5282